MW00931357

ADVENTURES
OF A TRAIL STOOGE

CHRIS QUINN

Copyright © 2015 Christopher Quinn

All rights reserved.

No part of this book may be used or reproduced in any
manner without written consent of the author, with the
exception of brief quotations within critical articles or reviews.

For information, email: chris@quinnwriter.com

ISBN: 1515279634
ISBN-13: 978-1515279631

Cover design by Paul Quinn

For more works by Chris Quinn, check out

www.quinnwriter.com

For more information on the Appalachian Trail, visit

www.appalachiantrail.org

Disclaimer

The following work has been created from personal perception
and memory. Conversations, names, defining characteristics,
events, and other details may not be as others see, or saw them.
As this is a work of perspective, everything is true, although it
may not be factual. My experience is formed by my own
memory and perception—my intention is solely to share that
experience here.

To Mom and Dad—thanks for everything.

Contents

Prologue

"It is no longer the atom which lives, but the universe within it."

—Pierre Teilhard de Chardin

Before the trail, I was in a good spot in life with nothing worthwhile to complain of. I had a good job, a good apartment, I lived in a good town. I was not an outdoorsman of any kind: I grew up in the suburbs with bikes, cars, and malls. The woods of my childhood were a thicket of trees that stood behind my neighborhood, large enough to get lost in only by imagination. But I grew up, and I found myself sitting at a desk day after day, pushing pencils and sending emails. But something pulled at my mind: unknown hands that demanded something more.

I believed my decision to thru-hike the AT was made by the powers of my own conscious reasoning. I told myself that it was for the thrill of adventure and the virtue of challenging oneself. People would ask me why I would leave behind a comfortable life for the trail, and a simple reason sung out: *I want to thru-hike. I want to challenge myself and see things I've never seen.* It was easy to answer that way. Nobody questioned me further.

But behind my confident, unobtrusive answer, there lay a hidden reason floating at the fringe of my mind. I could not utter a word about it, not for lack of courage, but for lack of knowledge of the essence of the *thing*. It was the hands of the true, hidden reason that pulled at me to start this walk. They pulled upon my mind, shaping it into something new, drawing it closer to a hidden mouth until, in a moment I can not recall and in a whisper too faint to notice, it spoke to me: *you are missing something vital—you are missing something that makes sense not by reason, but by spirit.*

I started the Appalachian Trail on May 7, 2013, hiking northbound from Georgia. I was twenty-five years old. Physically, it was an experience like none I've ever had. I, like many, tend to romanticize grand acts of physical endurance. When people like me never experience these things ourselves, we picture them as noble pursuits in which we conquer that which seems impossible.

But once I began to experience the reality of the trail, I saw that it was far from what I imagined. Instead of marching up mountains with the sun graciously shining upon my head, I found myself grasping for the last ounce of energy to make it off an exposed ridge in the pouring rain. Instead of daily baths in cool, clear waters, I found myself dirtied, smelly, tired, and curled up in an equally dirty and smelly tent. The images I held in my mind before my walk are not the ones I hold now.

I hoped, too, that this trip would open up my eyes to the riddles of the universe. I hoped that I would return with the insight of the Buddha and the knowledge of the cosmos. That I would find the mind of God, entering it through the gateway of nature. And that I would return a man of wisdom, shunning that which is valueless, and exuding peace and happiness from my very being. I set out on a search for an undefined, elusive *something*. In the pursuit of that hollow, lofty *something*, I failed miserably. I never had any blinding revelations—never experienced anything to claim as my moment of mystical awakening. But what I did find was a crevice, a foothold from which I could sometimes peer into the gaping void of a holy, pervasive *Nothingness*. From my small foothold, I could look upon the margin of the truth, and in some fleeting moments, gain the blessing of an indescribable knowledge. I found a different perspective of the world, myself, and those with whom we share the experience we call life.

I often struggle to keep that perspective. It sometimes slips away when I find myself worrying about my future success, my job, my finances, or just *my* place in the world. But when I find myself brooding over those things, I pull back on the string of my fading perspective and wrap it around my mind more tightly than ever. I cling to it because I know that that perspective, more simple and more beautiful than the one I applied to before, is a much truer representation of the world. On the trail, I lived a life untainted by the suffocating normalcy we bind ourselves with every day. I lived a much more lucid life—one free of restrictions imposed upon us by insignificant institutions and petty people. But more importantly, I was free of the restrictions that I imposed upon myself. I lived a life that was, in some transcendent moments, both entirely temporal and entirely eternal. I saw glimpses of something beautiful, and ultimately, I found a world of boundless love.

The following collection of journal entries will show what it was like for me on the trail. The romanticism of my pre-hike mind is tempered. What remains is the truth of the adventure—physically, mentally, and emotionally. It's the raw story of my trip along the collection of ground I've come to love: The Appalachian Trail.

I did my best to keep a running account of what I did each day, including places I went, people I met, and events that occurred; however, I did not keep the journal as meticulously as I wish I had. You will notice a wide range of issues: days being inaccurate (sometimes for weeks on end); ideas being incomplete or nebulous; the recording of events being postponed, sometimes for weeks at a time; unwarranted frustrations showing through the writing; and fatigue making itself known during the writing of my entries. I am not proud of each entry in this journal. I say some things that I wish I hadn't said, and I do some things I wish I hadn't done.

Despite these shortcomings, I have come to appreciate the journal for what it is. What I wrote was an accurate representation of my thoughts and feelings at that moment in time. No details that reflect badly on myself have been omitted. I did, however, feel it necessary to omit some details in order to protect certain other individuals. The omitted details are relatively minor, and I make note of the sections where the omissions occur.

Following each entry, I provide clarification and enhancement of the entry. These notes were added after the trail was completed and they seek to help the reader better understand the streaming nature of my thoughts in the associated journal entry. Through the notes, I attempt to make the rudimentary entries chronologically coherent and contextually relevant.

And lastly, please keep in mind that the following account is not meant to be read as a traditional narrative. Because it is a journal, there are bits of information that will be superfluous to the reader which don't add any substance to the story of my thru-hike. Please read this account simply for what it is at its core—the transparent thoughts and feelings of a twenty-five year old kid on a journey that would change his life.

Mile 1942.5

Had to get a new journal. Ran out of pages in the original. It's weird writing in this one. It's much nicer.

Right now I don't feel great. I'm missing home a bit and just want to get done with this trip. Paul left earlier today. It's always tough when someone visits or you go home. It's tough to get focused on the trail again. It was great having Paul out though—lots of fun. It just makes me miss home though.

I just put a rough plan together for the rest of the trip. Looks like I'll finish up right around the 10th or before. Before would be ideal. It's pretty weird to be planning for the end, even if it is preliminary planning. It's strange. It will be bittersweet. I'm ready for it to end, but I don't want to leave the trail. This trip has been such a mental game. I always tell people it's all mental. And when morale is low, it's rough.

I just don't know what I want. In some ways, I've figured things out, but I still am so confused about life, both mine + in general. I'm kind of scared for the future. This dread comes over me sometimes. Like it did before the trail as well. I think it's just part of who I am. I know there's so much to be excited + happy about, but sometimes, I just can't shake this damn dread.

Part I

"Every being has its own voice. Every being declares itself to the entire universe."

—Thomas Berry

Day 1 - May 7 2013

Hawk Mountain Shelter: 8.1

Day 1 was pretty intense. Woke up early (about 4:30) to catch my flight down to Atlanta. Mom + D brought me. I'm glad they were there to see me off. Mom did much better than I thought she would!

The trip to Atlanta was uneventful. Then Ron Brown picked me up + drove me to Springer. Ron is a pretty cool guy. He shuttles hikers all over the place, no matter the weather or time. He doesn't make much money, and he just lost his job as a Ranger, so that's tough. But he keeps shuttling people around. He does 3 am's to 12 midnights regularly. I asked how he stayed awake, and he said the energy from you guys, meaning hikers, which was cool. He's a good guy.

Anyway, hiked southbound to Springer a mile, then back down, then onward to Hawk Mountain Shelter, where I am now. It's about 8.5 miles along the trail. Not too bad for a half day.

I got some water, cooked, and now I'm writing. The food was mediocre at best. Knorr's Beef Pasta, and I put a little jerky in it. I didn't put enough fuel, so my pasta was very very el dente to say the least. Then I hung my food bag. Boom.

I must say, day 1 was pretty tough. This isn't going to be easy at all. There have been a couple times where I think if I can do it or not. Honestly, it's tough. It rained right when I got into camp, the trails were wet all day from last night's rain. My feet were soaked. Then I had to cook in the rain, then put my food bag up in the rain. The rain is going to be real tough I think.

Ron told me I need to get a permit to hike through the Smokies, in Georgia. I need to get that + print it out. I'm pretty tired. I think it's like 8. I may turn in for the night.

May 7 Notes: I left my home in South Jersey on the morning of May 7, 2013. My father saw me off at home. Mom and my sister Danielle drove me to the Philadelphia airport. After saying our goodbyes, I left Mom and Danielle at the security check and walked to my gate. I sat down and pulled a letter from my pocket. It was from my Mom and Dad. I pulled back tears and tucked it away in my small carry on. Twenty minutes later, I boarded the plane.

As I planned my thru-hike, my father was my confidant: I shared my fears and hopes with him. But my mother was worried and upset by my decision to hike the trail. I may have had little idea what to expect, but my Mom thought I'd be fighting off bears and murderers while bushwhacking the Eastern seaboard. Luckily, I did none of those things, and I came back alive. Although it annoyed me at times, I understood her concern. And I loved her more deeply for it.

Aside from my support at home, there was support on the trail. There are many people associated with the Appalachian Trail community who help thru-hikers along the way. They are commonly called Trail Angels—individuals who offer services to hikers, some at a price and some for free. One such person was Ron Brown. I had called Ron a few days before I left for Atlanta to set up his shuttling service from the Atlanta Airport to Springer Mountain, about a two hour drive. Ron dropped me off at the small parking lot at the base of Springer Mountain. He doled out several ounces of denatured alcohol into a plastic bottle, handed it to me, then left. I hiked south one mile to reach the summit, from which I would officially begin my thru-hike. It took a day of high-speed, modern travel, but I was finally away from the urban locales of Philadelphia and Atlanta. Puddles dotted the trail, trees rose in my vision, dirt was beneath my feet. I climbed atop Springer, the southern terminus of the Appalachian Trail, and looked out over miles of untamed land.

Another hiker summited Springer from the south, having hiked through Amicalola Falls State Park. He was young, and his restrained nervous energy fought to free itself from his body. His glasses seemed out of place on his large frame, and he wore a Detroit Tigers visor and big hiking boots. *Hey,* I said. *Hey. How are you? You thru-hiking?* He dropped his pack and took a drink. *Yea, just started from the lot down there, so my pack is at the bottom waiting for me.* He was sweating. *Man, I came*

9

through Amicalola. I just walked up so many steps. It wasn't too fun. He laughed. I looked at the plaque that marks the start of the trail. A bronze man hikes upward: *A Footpath for Those who seek Fellowship with the Wilderness.* I pulled out my phone and called my mother to tell her I was off. I hung up with crying coming through from the other end of the line. I turned off my phone, picked up my poles, and hiked back down Springer. My thru-hike had begun.

Day 2 - May 8 2013
Gooch Gap Shelter: 15.8

Last night's sleep was pretty rough. I slept like crap. I woke up + tossed + turned til about 3am I think. I had some wild half dreams, none of which I can recall. But they were strange. I was cold + hot intermittently as well. But oh well, crappy nights will happen.

Today was great though. I hauled about 10 miles in 4 hours. I finished up at about 1pm here at Gooch Gap Shelter. I'll rest here the rest of the day, and load up for my push through the bear/no camp zone. I'll need to rip about 15 miles tomorrow, which I don't think will be too bad. I need to get through Neels Gap tomorrow though.

I met some cool people the last couple of days. Four recent college grads from Florida have been walking at somewhat my pace the past two days. I think they're coming into camp right now actually. All cool dudes. I got a picture of them. I also met a man and his sister, around 50, who are sort of attempting a thru hike. They know they won't make it, but they're just going to keep going. I think they can make it—I hope they do.

Then I met a cool dude from NJ today, whose name is Stay Puffed. He's a bigger dude from North Jersey. Super nice, super normal. He gave himself the name Stay Puffed because he's big, white, and from the city—like the Ghost Buster's marshmallow man. It's a good name. Some dude tried to give me the name "Soon" today because he asked me if I had a trail name and I said "No. Hopefully soon." So he said "Why not Soon?" I kind of laughed, then we parted ways. So I hope that's not my trail name, it's whack. I don't want to name myself though either. So we'll see.

The views out here are pretty awesome, especially when you're on a mountain + can look down over a gap + another mountain. But mostly it's a lot of trees. It's beautiful though still.

As I was talking to Stay Puffed, he mentioned I can get that Smokie Mt. permit at the Ranger station right before you go in. So I'll probably do that.

I'm going to make a little fire right now—but I did not.

Later that day. Today was pretty sweet. I hung out a lot, cooked and ate. I made oatmeal (delicious), Ramen (delicious), and a tuna packet. I'll resupply at Neels Gap tomorrow. I need to get there early though. I hear there are only 16 beds at the place I want to stay at.

Met a few new people today. Lea + Larry (Larry tried to give me the trail name "Soon.") Mike, who is pretty funny + seems like a cool dude, and a young couple, but I forget their names right now.

We all hung out tonight, ate, talked. It was a fun time.

And I almost forgot this other guy named Steve. Older man, really nice. He's not going thru, he's just shooting for Hot Springs.

This shelter is cool. It's Gooch Gap Shelter. There are a bunch of terraced campsites surrounding the shelter, so I'm on one of them. The shelter itself is supposed to suck—rats + such.

Non event talk: I'm surprised how much weight people are carrying around. I'm at like 26 and I want lower. People are lugging around 45-50 pound packs. It's insane. No wonder people aren't moving more quickly. They're super weighed down. Ron said the average weight he's seeing jumped this year to almost 50. The previous years, it had been dropping. I wonder why it jumped so high this year—kind of weird.

Looks like tonight's crew is all shooting for Neels Gap tomorrow. That will be fun if we make it. Night.

May 8 Notes: In the early days of my journey, I was figuring out what I was doing in the most basic sense. It quickly dawned on me that I was in fact walking many miles through woods, eating terrible food, and meeting a bunch of random people. On top of the strangeness of that situation, I had no idea what I was doing with regard to the practice of hiking. I had to ask what to do with my trash. Stay Puffed gave me an extra plastic shopping bag that he had—my first trash bag. I kept that one for about a quarter of the trail. The bag lasted me quite a while, but unfortunately, I never saw Stay Puffed again.

The couple whose names I could not remember was Eli and Rachel (aka Cannon and Lady). They were a young, enthusiastic couple who had spent the previous year down in the US Virgin Islands. They had the subtle, laid back look of islander transplants and the demeanor to go with it. Alongside Eli's camera equipment, they carried freeze dried meals that became the stuff of legend—no Ramen or pop tarts for them. Eli was a stout guy with broad square feet that browned in his open topped sandals. I always thought he was crazy for wearing them. Rachel was a pretty girl who was always there to share a laugh or smile.

Mike later took the trail name Tangy Booch Magoo, or simply Tangy. It didn't seem like it, but Tangy was in his thirties. He acted like he was fifteen, but not in a bad way. His short, red hair was true to his free spirited nature, and his small glasses gave him an air of wisdom. But his wisdom always came in the form of a sharp joke or a witty comment: he was a professor of good-willed deprecation, the fool who always showed us our flaws.

The Detroit-visored kid I met atop Springer was also there this night, although I did not mention him in the entry. His name was Matt, but he eventually went by the trail name Munchies. The beginning of the trail is strange in the way you make friends so easily. The prospect of a long journey binds you together quickly. Tangy and Munchies became good friends. They were my first friends. But on the trail, friends are easy to lose too.

Day 3 - May 9

Neels Gap: 31.7

Did 15 today. It was a long day. I'll write more info tomorrow.

Today is the tenth. But I'll write here. So the 9th was the longest day so far. About 15 miles. I started fairly early + ended at 5:15 at Mountain Crossings in Neels Gap. I went up + over Blood Mountain. Some great views up there, but the descent was terrible. I hiked the whole day alone + made some good time. But my feet paid a price, a couple of blisters.

I stayed the night at the hostel. There was a hilarious thru hiker there who we named Hostel Talker. I think everyone knows his life story. Anyway, he was hilarious + strange.

At 6:00, some church group served us burgers + baked potatoes! Awesome timing since they only do it once a year. I gorged on a burger, veggie burger, + a huge potato. Right after eating, Munchies + Tangy showed up. Luckily there were some leftovers. Then we just chilled + some crazy old guy named Inch Worm showed up. He talked like crazy too. The hostel was funny too. Super dirty, cats just hanging out all over, and some guy named Pirate ran it. He was old. It was a really cool place though, I'm glad I stayed there.

May 9 Notes: As I descended Blood Mountain, I took a short rest. I sat in the middle of the trail, my back resting on a fallen log. A bug crawled on the earth beside me. The skies were open. White tufts of cloud hung lazily at arm's length. My blister pain melted away. For the first time, I felt aligned both within and without.

In contrast, I took my first blundering fall the day before. I slid down a small muddy slope and fell right on my butt: hiking poles clanging against rock, mud streaks down my legs. Tangy and Munchies, hiking directly behind me, got a good laugh out of it. Falls are expected on the trail, so getting my first one out of the way was a relief. But despite the contrasting emotions of my euphoric alignment on Blood

Mountain and my clumsy fall, something subtle tied them together: a willingness to accept them at what they were.

Hostel Talker was an overweight man of about forty with curly dark hair. He wore an exuberant aspect, but he seemed emotionally exhausted, like he was talking about nothing in order to keep from talking about something. He was taking a few zeros (a zero is a day off) in Neels Gap, gathering his mental faculties before hitting the trail again. His previous attempt at a thru-hike earlier in the season had been a disaster. His cheap butane stove sprung a leak and exploded, resulting in minor burns to his hands. The weather, for which he was ill prepared, was frigid. He decided to call off the attempt and go live with his sister for a month while he healed up physically and mentally. Tangy, Munchies, another hiker named Scott, and I hiked out the next morning. I doubt Hostel Talker ever resumed his thru-hike from Neels Gap.

Day 4 - May 10

Low Gap Shelter: 43.2

My allergies are killing me. They won't go away. Sleeping is a pain. During the day when I'm hiking it's not too bad. But night time is not the right time.

Me, Munchies + Tangy all hiked together today. It was only 11 miles, but it felt like 20. My feet were pretty banged up, the blisters popped on the hike. But nothing too terrible. We took a lot of breaks today, too many, which made the day really too long.

I like those dudes, but not sure if I can stick with them, I won't make Katahdin. Dude named Scott was with us today too, but he came into camp maybe an hour after.

I'm in my tent now and these birds are singing to each other. One sounds like he's in a tree right next to me, it's cool. We're at Low Gap Shelter tonight. Scott just posted up like 5 feet from my tent. Little weird, but he is.

I've been sleeping terribly. Getting into bed at a decent

hour, but not really getting to sleep until like 2am. Then I sleep til 7 or whatever. It's partially allergies and partially tent sleeping. Oh well, hopefully it gets better.

I talked to Mom + D last night. Mom did good. Started to cry just a little bit as we said goodbye. But she was excited for me. I liked that. And D sounded good too. I do miss everyone though. It's a little weird being so dislocated. But this is what I wanted.

I may go into town in the next few days. So I may be able to update the blog then. I have a few good topics to write on as well as my trip's summary so far. I'm going to sleep now. Ah, forgot one thing. I have the start of a trail name. It started as Barkley (Charles Barkley) because Tangy thought I said "terrible" a lot. Then it changed to Sir Charles Gouloins (your balls) because Tangy liked when I called balls gools. But now I want Stooge involved in it somewhere. So I'm trying for Sir Stooge Goulons. But Tangy still wants Charles involved in it somewhere. So we'll see where it ends up tomorrow! Alright time for bed! Night.

May 10 Notes: All four of us had a rough day, Munchies especially. He wore big, heavy boots and he blistered up a lot. His knees were also giving him trouble. He was wetting handkerchiefs in streams and wrapping them around his legs in an attempt to alleviate the swelling and pain. Tangy, always the joker, reminded Munchies that a soggy handkerchief around a knee does little for the knee's pain.

Scott took the name Nine Nails due to injuries sustained on the trail. One of his toe nails came off from trauma. Two days later, he would go by the name Eight Nails for obvious reasons.

I tended to my blistered feet, happy to be free from any serious injury, yet worried about the possibility of one. The threat of injury and pain was ever present on the trail: sometimes it was dark and overbearing, other times it was light and distant. But I also worried about intangible injury: the weakness of my will to thru-hike. When I told people I was hiking the AT, they would almost always ask, *The whole thing?* I'd tell them that I was *trying* to thru-hike. With that statement,

I insulated myself from the threat of bodily and moral injury. I was a ghost hiker, walking painful miles without resolve, afraid of looking like a fool if I went home early: so I just said I was trying. And at Low Gap Shelter, trying seemed pretty brutal. As Munchies struggled with his knees and Nine Nails lost toenails, I repressed the urge to stop walking. But deep in my mind I knew I could quit the trail and be done with it: a finality both freeing and devastating.

Day 5 - May 11

Cheese Factory Site: 56.6

I'm at the Cheese Factory! This camp site was apparently an old cheese factory. I haven't had a chance to look around. Me + Tangy got here about 5, set up tent quickly, and a storm rolled in around 5:15. It's now 6:30. We're waiting the storm out so we can get water + cook something. It's not looking great though.

Today we did about 14. Munchies + Nine Nails headed into town at Unicoi Gap, about 4 miles back. Me and Tangy are going to awaken early tomorrow, hike to Dicks Gap, then hitch into town to watch some hockey. We need to wake up super early though.

Today's hike really wasn't too eventful. It was pretty tough though. I'm glad I made it to the Cheese Factory. Now we only have about 14 into Dicks Creek Gap.

My name is now Sir Stooge Charles Guilons. But I'm going to sign in at shelters as variants of such. Like "The Esteemed Stooge, Sir Guilons." Or "Stooge Premier, Sir Charles Guilons." Or "Your Grand Stooginess, Sir Charles Guilons." Should be fun.

This rain stinks. But I think it's almost passed. And I smell pretty bad I think. Pretty bad.

This is a little later on. Rain stopped, got water + cooked. Made Ramen with some chunks of sausage jerky stuff in it. Not bad at all. Now about ready to hop in bed.

Me + Tangy were just talking about Nine Nails. I think I already said that he broke his back in college jumping off a second story balcony. So he's about 35, and his broken back really messed him up. Can't really feel his lower body. So it's really impressive that he's doing the trail. He has his grandpa's staff now, but he's probably getting trekking poles while he's in town. He needs them. I asked him why he's doing the AT. And it's cool. He said he's doing it because he always told his dad he would. His dad passed away last year. And he's also doing it for a friend who just died of brain cancer. So for every mile, he's raising money for that. Pretty neat. He's a quiet dude, but he's pretty legit.

Anyway, I'm going to turn in now. Tomorrow is going to be early. Night.

May 11 Notes: I eventually dropped the title variations of my trail name and took the official name of "The Esteemed Stooge, Sir Charles Guilons." My friends commonly referred to me as Sir Stooge, or simply as Stooge. The pronunciation of Guilons is *gool-yohns*. I never spelled the word out in my life until the trail. It's not one often used in print. Trail names are taken by nearly every thru-hiker on the trail and they often become the only means by which others are known. Of my many friends on the trail, I know the real names of only a few. But that doesn't make them any less personal. Trail names are not a way to hide your true self or conceal a dark past: they are only names, and a name is not a person.

There were many common hiking practices that I was completely unaware of. While at the Cheese Factory, I realized my bear bag technique had been comically wrong the previous several nights. After we ate, Tangy and I found a good tree from which to hang our bear bags. He watched as I tied my line to my food bag (sometimes as much as ten pounds or so), and lined myself up by facing away from the branch upon which I was to hang my bag from. I then loaded up with a swing between my legs before launching the bear bag backwards and over my head—all the while hoping it would reach the waiting branch above.

As my bag swung violently from the branch, Tangy

smiled easily and asked, *What the hell are you doing?* He patiently explained to me that it was much easier to tie a rock to the end of the line, throw the rock over the branch, then simply hoist the bag up. *Oh damn,* I laughed. *That way is much easier.*

I never saw Nine Nails again. I don't know if he completed his thru-hike or if he left the trail soon after. His back injury severely hindered his hiking ability, and what to an average hiker was a difficult journey was made all the more difficult for him. I never got to know him well, but I suspect the spoken reason for his journey, his father's and friend's deaths, was not the entire story. There is an unspoken reason that each individual hikes the trail, the whisper that we barely hear. For Nine Nails, I never found out what that was. I'm not sure if he did either.

Day 6 May 12 - Mother's Day
Dicks Creek Gap: 69.6

It's about 2 PM and I'm at Dick's Creek Gap. I arrived a few minutes ago and am just waiting on Tangy. As I was waiting I talked to a nice old lady who was waiting for her daughter + son in law. They took her out to search for wild flowers. She's too old to walk in the hills though, so she was just waiting in the gap. Nice lady though, she was funny.

We hauled pretty good today. Started about 7:15 and finished about 2, I think about 15 miles. I like morning hiking best. It's more refreshing. And you can see the sun start low and rise. And there's fog + dew heavy in the air. It seems clean + nice. Today was pretty chilly too. Definitely the coldest day so far. I wore both shirts all day.

The hike was good. A couple ascents + descents of about 1,000 feet. Fun hiking day. Now I just want to get into town. About a half mile from the gap, a sketchy Georgian guy was standing there with his dog. Really heavy drawl, and smoking a cig. He talked to me for a minute, and offered a ride to Hiawassee. I don't know if I want it though. He weirded me out. I thought it might be Red Pickup Guy, but there's no red pickup in the lot here. I hope Tangy gets in here soon. I want to get out of here.

I think I flew the last 5 miles. I got a nice runner's high going uphill the first mile, then just rode it out. I took 2 very short breaks. I hope I didn't leave Tangy too far behind. That weird guy on the trail makes me nervous too.

May 12 Notes: The old woman was sitting on a stone bench when I first arrived at the gap. I took a seat on some steps about twenty feet from her. She was grey and serene, a fairy mother that had been sent to me on Mother's Day. I can't recall what we talked about, but it was comforting. It reminded me of home. Her son-in-law and daughter came down out of the hills a few minutes later. But for those few minutes, she was my mother.

Hikers are a vulnerable group. Sometimes there are individuals who will try to take advantage of that fact. The Red Pickup Guy I mention was a man (although it was not the Georgian with a cigarette I encountered) who would offer hikers a ride into town. He would play the role of good samaritan: chatting, questioning, and smiling as he drove. But after a mile or two, he forced the hikers out of his truck and he drove away with their gear, likely to sell it off somewhere. Hearing of people like him was more depressing than frightening. Thankfully, I'd come to find out that people like Red Pickup Guy were rare.

Day 7 - May 13th

GA/NC Border: 78.5

I'll pick up from where I left off the last entry. Tangy was fine, he was just a little behind. We hitched a ride pretty easily with some old native Hiawassee guy. He was coming back from fishing. He caught one really small trout. He was funny because he knew it was too tiny and he's not sure why he didn't release it.

We got into Hiawassee. Little town with almost nothing to do. We ate McDonald's (delicious) and got a room at the Holiday Inn Express. It was nice having a long shower and a bed. We had to then take a cab to go to one of the few open bars, it was all the way in North Carolina! The cab cost $45 which sucked. I tried to get him down to $30 on phone, and he rejected. Then when we got in the car, he told me he didn't like when people tried to "jew" him down. His words—hilarious. He wound up being nice though.

The bar we went to was hilarious. It was just me and Tangy. We watched some playoff hockey, ate, drank, then went home. When the cabbie came to get us (we got a round trip deal), he also made a drug deal with some dude at the bar—hilarious. Overall, fun, but strange night. Hiawassee sucks.

I updated my blog which was cool. I put a trip update, and a post about siblings. I think they were both decent.

So that brings me to today's hike. I'll say it was the worst hiking day I've had. My lower legs are killing me. Right in my achilles area. I was just massaging them, and I feel a little bump on my right achilles—I don't like that. We did about 10 miles after getting a late jump out of town—we hit the trail like 2:30 and finished like 6:00. Four young dudes from Tennessee gave us a ride to the gap. They were going camping too, but somewhere way down the road. I think they were all in a church group—nice guys though.

My alcohol stove is busted. It leaks out of the bottom. I was wondering why I was going through so much alcohol. Now I only have like 4 oz left for about a week's journey. That sucks. I need to do some surgery on it tomorrow, then either make or buy something at the NOC. I'm a little nervous about my alcohol though. I can always cook over a fire, so it's not a huge deal, just a pain.

I'm going to turn in now since it's a little late. I need to do some leg massaging, then sleep. Smell ya's later.

May 13 Notes: Tangy and I thumbed a ride into Hiawassee, the first hitch of my life. I spoke ill of the town, but it was more than "a little town with almost nothing to do." It was quiet and easy: the silent hum of a Sunday in a small Bible Belt town. At the hotel, Tangy and I made the best of our time: we resupplied, printed out our Smokie Mountain permits, and went in the pool. Tangy washed his feet with soap and a wash cloth in the hot tub. It was gross. Then we went through my first hiker box in the lobby of the Holiday Inn. Hiker boxes are just containers full of things that other hikers have no need for or don't want anymore. You'll find food, gear, and some other worthwhile items in there. Most hotels and hostels will have some type of hiker box. But getting good stuff is always difficult: the good stuff gets taken immediately while the bad stuff builds up over time. The one in the Holiday Express was decent. I took a bunch of tampons for tinder as well as some meal bars and other food.

Nine Nails and Munchies were also in Hiawassee that night, but they didn't come to the bar with us. We didn't have Nine Nails' number, and Munchies' cell phone service was terrible. They wound up splitting a room at another motel in Hiawassee. Munchies got bed bugs. He had to deal with that, fumigating them from his gear and body. And he rested, nursing his knees to health. That took time. He was a good friend, but I did not want to wait for him. By the time the morning was over on May 13, I was ready to get back on the trail again. I didn't fly to Georgia to stay in a hotel. I flew down to try to hike the Appalachian Trail. I wanted the struggle again.

Day 8 - May 14th

Carter Gap Shelters: 93.9

Good news is that my alcohol stove doesn't leak, I think I just had a bad pour. I didn't use it tonight though since I only have a few ounces of alcohol left. So I built a little fire + cooked on that. It worked pretty well, so I was happy. I used a tampon as tinder—it worked awesomely. I should have taken more from that hiker box.

I may make some oatmeal in the morning—using the alcohol stove to save time + effort. We shall see.

Today's hike was some good, some bad. I started off feeling fine, but around mile 9, my left achilles was killing me. I had to stop + wrap it. My achilles are making me nervous. I hope they are ok. Me + Tangy hiked together the first leg, then I left him tagging on the second leg. He got into the shelter pretty late, but he made dinner on the trail.

Sorry, side tracked. My left started hurting around mile 8, but then stopped at about 12 or so. So I'm hoping that's good. I'm tired, almost falling asleep writing. Today was a pretty mild day overall.

May 14 Notes: The pain in my legs tightened my strides and swelled my ankles. It was in both legs, intermittently, on the lower backside near my Achilles tendon. For the most part, it was not so much pain as it was severe discomfort and excessive tightness. Sometimes even that would go away for hours at a time. But every once in a while, without any real reason, I would get a searing line of hot pain that shot upward through my Achilles into my lower calf. Several times I buckled in my gait. I was hurt, and I knew it. I was afraid of what my injury could mean for the future of my hike.

Day 9 - May 15th
Licklog Gap: 122.1

Today is actually the 16th, but I didn't write last night. I honestly can't remember much from yesterday besides my left achilles being in pain at some points.

I was (and still am) babying them, but sometimes I'd get a quick, shooting pain in my left achilles. Not cool.

May 15 Notes: The pain in my legs was never severe enough to keep me from hiking, but I often thought that I was making it worse by not stopping. With nearly every step, my mind imagined how painful a ruptured Achilles tendon would be. I reverted to walking like a lead-footed monster: stepping toward earth with my back upright and my legs stiff and straight below me. My unyielding heels met the earth first in order to keep the load off my tendon and calf. I walked like a steampunk robot who had his leg joints fused together. With each blundering step, I hoped that I would be spared a searing shot of pain. But even more so, I hoped that my tendon would not explode under the weight of my pack.

Day 10 - May 16th

Licklog Gap: 122.1

Anyway, my legs are getting better. My left felt great. My right started to hurt a little bit though. I have it wrapped since it looked like I had a tiny bit of swelling.

But I'll tell you why it hurts now, because it was fine most of the day.

We woke up at the campsite. We camped right next to a stream with 3 other hikers. They were nice. Two 18 year olds + a 24. All cousins. This morning, the 18 year old dude interviewed me about my hike. It was funny. So we wake up + start hiking. All goes well until about mile 10. At mile 10, there's a sign at a fork in the trail. To the left is "Shelter — .25 mi" and it shows nothing to the right. I turned right—bad news bears. We traveled about 2 miles before getting to a landmark that wasn't in our guide—we were on the wrong trail. Probably burned 4 or 5 miles of unneeded trail. It sucked. But we recovered, even though we're camping 3 miles short of where we intended to. Oh well.

So my leg hurts from all the running around + back tracking we did because of that screw up. Tangy was a little mad, as was I, but we figured it out. Just sucks anyway.

It's 8:30 now, and I'm pretty exhausted from that debacle. Only 15 miles to NOC though, so we're going to knock that out starting early tomorrow morning.

May 16 Notes: As I made my way back to the fork in the trail after hiking those unnecessary miles, I felt like I was back at square one after accomplishing nothing. A few hours prior, after making the ill advised turn, it took Tangy and I around a mile before we became suspicious that we were doing something wrong. After going another half mile, and seeing Tangy's growing frustration, I made a wry joke about how we were on the "wrong trail" in an attempt to cut the growing tension. We soon found ourselves in Grasshopper Gap #2, a landmark that is *not* on the Appalachian Trail. Luckily I had service. I took out my phone and discovered we were on the Benton MacKaye Trail. We made the demoralizing trek back to the Appalachian Trail and spent the night at Lick Log Gap, several miles short of our planned mileage for the day. It was a trying experience, but we came out fine in the end. At Lick Log Gap we laughed. I heartily cursed the trail markings, all the while knowing that the real blame lie with myself.

Ripsock, the young interviewer, took out his small camera and asked me a few questions. *Name? Chris Quinn also known as The Esteemed Stooge Sir Charles Guilons. And where are you from? Mount Laurel, New Jersey. And why are you thru-hiking the trail?* I thought about it. I still didn't understand why I was doing it. I settled for the answer that would be easy to explain. *I just want to challenge myself, meet new people. You know, just see new stuff.* He moved on. *And what's the most important piece of advice that you would share with someone thinking about hiking the AT?* I kept my answer short: *Pack light.* Besides a light pack making hiking physically easier, it makes life mentally simpler. Thru-hikers carry only what they need, not what they want. I had already ditched some unnecessary items, but this lesson was still being learned. I still carried a two-pound tomahawk on the side of my pack. It was a glorified hammer. I staked my tent in with the butt-end every night.

I wish I had added a second piece of advice to Ripsock's interview: *Enjoy each moment, no matter the circumstances. That moment is all we ever have.* After chronicling my Benton MacKaye debacle on my blog, I received a message from a former high school classmate and former AT thru-hiker, Brandon

"Monkey" Imp. He told me to play the "At Least" game. At least I wasn't above tree line in a storm. At least I only had to hike two miles back to the AT instead of twenty. At least I wasn't sitting behind a desk, pushing pencils and sending emails. I was on the trail, out in the woods, seeing new things, meeting spectacular people. I was actively creating a new mindframe that demanded my physical, mental, and spiritual faculties. Even during the challenges and tribulations, I was doing something transformative—all I had to do was realize it.

Day 11 + 12 - May 17th + 18th
Nantahala Outdoor Center: 137.3

Made it to the NOC. This place is great. I'm actually writing this on the 19th because the NOC was so much fun I didn't have time to write.

So the 15 miles to the NOC felt long! I think this is when I saw the rattlesnake too. But we made it. We grabbed a room at the "hostel," which they called Basecamp. It was not really a hostel, it was more like a bunch of small buildings that contained 4 or 5 small rooms each. Only furnished with beds + a fan.

We spent the first night eating awesome barbecue + crushing beers. It was a good time. On the 18th, we took a zero. We ate + drank more of course. We resupplied + I got a second Ace bandage. Now I have one for each foot! I also updated my blog + made some calls. I talked to Mom + Dad, Neil, and Steve Reynolds. Steve may move to San Fran soon. Crazy. So it was a good day to get caught up + resupplied. The rest also helped my achy legs too.

Tangy got a pizza for lunch, then carried a few slices with him on the trail—great move. I should have pulled that. I got a burger, salad + tater tots though. It was all delicious. Can't wait to get into town again to crush food.

So the zero day was fun. I like the NOC. It's a cool place.

Ripsock, Songbird, + Sunshine were there on our zero as well. So we hung with them that night. Ripsock was being funny. He's getting a little frustrated just hanging with those 2 girls. So he was hanging with me + Tangy a lot.

May 17 + 18 Notes: The trail looped, turned, and descended. I could hear moving water and cars. I knew I was near the Nantahala Outdoor Center—the NOC. Sitting astride the Nantahala River, the NOC has rafting, zip lining, an outfitter, a small resupply, and several restaurants. Tangy and I quickly washed up and headed to a restaurant with an outdoor seating area. We didn't move from there all night. I was off of my feet with a beer in my hand and food on my plate.

Ripsock, Songbird, and Sunshine, the three cousins we camped with the previous night, came into the NOC later that day. Ripsock was a goofy eighteen year old just starting to find his own personality. He was going through all the awkward worries of high school—acne and his looks, his friends and girls, and just being cool. Tangy and I told him that we were there once too—acne and all. S*top caring what others think or what they think you should be or look like*, I told him. *You're your own person.* I acted as though it were so simple to do, but I knew it wasn't. It took me twenty-five years just to start to become my own person and think my own way. Just to decide that I wanted to do something different, to walk a trail instead of sit behind a desk. Twenty five years just to make a choice to seek something that I wanted for myself, yet was beyond myself. But I still didn't even consider myself a thru-hiker. I was still just giving it all a try. And even in deciding to hike the trail, was it solely my own decision? I had so much input from friends and family along the way. Their thoughts and feelings mixed with mine because I care about them and they about me. Our minds and hearts don't work in a vacuum, and I failed to see that with Ripsock and his high school struggles. It's easy to tell people how to live when you aren't them. It all seems so simple from the outside. But no matter how hard we try, we can't extricate ourselves from the rest of life. There would be nothing left. *Each perspective has an equal and opposite re-perspective.* But Ripsock seemed to enjoy the conversation: perhaps it's good to get advice even when it's too difficult to live by. Tangy got up to get us a beer. Ripsock refused the offer but followed Tangy to refill his soda.

Tangy returned with a cider for Songbird and a beer for me. Songbird was in her mid twenties. She was short and cheerful. But like many hikers, she was searching for something unspoken. She was cool and calm, as easy to talk to as she was easy to be silent with. Later on, she would send me an occasional text after catching up on my journey through my blog. She became enthralled with my trip, and I was happy to have her involved in it. Songbird became my cheerleader, sending messages of encouragement as she pushed me northward, but I never saw her again after the NOC.

Support came from other places too, both on the trail and from home. I spoke with Steve Reynolds, a good college buddy of mine. I also called Steve Olson (aka Scuba Springsteen) while at the NOC. Steve thru-hiked the AT in 2012. It was really Scuba Springsteen who got me to seriously consider a thru-hike. He was the one who gave me advice and tips on how to pack, what to do, where to stop, and everything between. He even gave all of my gear a run through before I left for the trail. On the phone, we didn't talk about anything special, just a bunch of reminiscing about his thru-hike the previous year.

Scuba Springsteen said he wished he was out on the trail again. But he was happy that I was doing it: *an equal and opposite re-perspective*. I thought about how Scuba Springsteen had hiked the whole trail, and I thought about all the other people who had done the same. I thought about what I told Ripsock: *Be your own person. Who cares what others think you should be or what you should do.* I needed to stop caring about what everyone would think if I came home early. But I also needed to see that they were an integral part of my experience. I had to find a lightness of mind that allowed for a depth of will. At the NOC, I realized that I wasn't just *trying* to hike the AT. I was *doing* it. I was a thru-hiker.

Day 13 - May 18th

Brown Fork Gap Shelter: 153.1

Getting back on the trail after a zero is mentally difficult. But physically it's great. My legs + body felt so much better after a day of rest. It was much needed.

We did about fifteen today to Brown Fork Gap Shelter. Pretty uneventful though. Except for the awesome part when I saw cows chilling on the AT. It was hilarious. I turned a corner + I see 2 or 3 cows eating + hanging. And they had 3 babies with them. Not sure how the cows got there, but they were. They weren't moving, so I had to go into the trees to get around them. It was hilarious.

I'm falling asleep as I'm writing. I should go.

May 18 Notes: In all, the discomfort and pain in my Achilles tendons lasted about ten days. After some research, I diagnosed myself with acute tendonitis of the Achilles tendons. I began a regimen of NSAIDs and compression to treat the symptoms. Each morning, I would wake and wrap my ankles in compression bandages and swallow two NSAIDs. I eventually stopped wrapping my ankles although I religiously took the NSAIDs every morning.

These two treatments reduced the swelling, and the searing shots of pain soon stopped. The tightness and discomfort subsided over several days as the anti-inflammatories took full effect. My legs soon came alive as the tension fell out of them. I was free to support my full weight on my forefoot. I no longer needed to strike the earth with my heel in order to keep pressure from running up the band of my Achilles and into my calf. I hiked with a lightness I hadn't felt since the start of the trail. The mechanisms of my foot and lower leg were working once again, flexing and contracting in an amazing orchestra of muscle, bone, and tendon.

Day ? - May 22

Double Spring Gap Shelter: 196.0

So I have no idea what happened to my day count. Today is May 22 though. Let's see what happened since the cows.

This is the second day in the Smokies. So I'll recount from the start of the Smokies. The day before we entered the Smokies I camped about a mile from the Visitor Center at a little campsite. Tangy brought some canned margaritas from the dock, about 3 miles before the campsite. I came really close to going down there to swim too. Dang! Wish I went down there! I could have gotten some drinks + swam, and I was only about 15 min in front of Tangy too. He crushed a few there, then brought some to the campsite. So at least I got about one and a half!

So the next day, I went down to Fontana Dam Visitor Center nice + early so I could get some food then hit the trail. Unfortunately, the snack shop never opened at its proposed 10am time. But, I got some sweet Trail Magic. The old lady who worked at the Dam's Visitor Center saw me waiting for the shop to open up. She gave me some Vienna Sausages + an apple. It was awesome! Me + Tangy split them. Those were my first Vienna Sausages. So even though I didn't get in the shop, it was a nice breakfast.

The rest of the day was decent. It rained a bit toward the end as I came into the shelter. Due to Smokies rules, I tried sleeping in the shelter. It was terrible—people scuffling + snoring + stuff.

I left camp about 6:15 am because I couldn't take the shelter. Today's hike was pretty decent. Did 17 miles + am now at the shelter. I met this cool dude named Cedric who I've been hiking with most of the day. He's a white Native American. I forget his tribe—in Oklahoma though. His mom is native, dad is Norwegian. He looks full white though. Cool dude though.

Over the past 2 days I've been in comm with Mom +

Dad to ready for Celli's bachelor party. I'm going to hike to Erwin, TN, then get into Johnson City, TN where I'll rent a car. Then I'll drive to Nashville for the week/weekend. Since I have the car Wednesday, I can pick Matt + Paul + whoever else up at the airport which is good. I'm super excited for Nashville. It's going to rock!!!

May 22 Notes: It was tough for me to keep days straight while I was on the trail. I easily lost track of days, dates, and time in general. Time did not seem to pass consistently and concretely. Instead, it flowed like water, surging quickly past or lulling in a still pool. Weeks no longer became a worthwhile unit of measurement as I was set free from the seven day cycle. Days were no longer parts of a month or made up of hours—they were simply single units of light and dark. As you'll soon see from my entries, I lost track of the months as well. I no longer knew the changing of seasons by the month of the year, but by the feel of the air and earth around me, by the temperature and the trees. This all happened subtly and without effort. In the modern world, it would perhaps be an intellectual regression to lose track of the labels imposed upon natural processes. But on the trail, it was a spiritual progression. Life is not made for measuring.

May 23

Newfound Gap: 206.8

I'm sitting here at Newfound Gap. It's a bit of a tourist site here. I guess it's a nice view on the way to Clingman's Dome. And you can get to some trails from here. It's funny—whenever you're at these touristy spots, people just ask you if you're thru hiking. It's pretty neat. I just talked to some crazy old lady who went on a rant about humans being stupid and one of the few animals who fight to the death. It started as a conversation about wildlife—weird.

This morning was a little disappointing. I got to

Clingman's Dome around 10, but there was no view—too overcast. I waited around for an hour or so, but no soup for me. Oh well.

I did get a few awesome granola bars at the visitor's center as well as some cured pork. I planned on lunching on the cured meat, however, after my first bite, I was rather alarmed. I looked at the packaging and apparently you still need to cook it even though it's cured. It was pretty much raw. If cured at all, it was to the minimum. I'm going to fry a little up tonight though and put it in some Ramen.

The Smokies have been cool. Weather is overcast, but the forest is neat. It's been the first coniferous stuff I've seen. So it's nice.

Three more miles to Ice Water Shelter, then dinner!

So I'm about to go to sleep—but there are two stories. Firstly, Cedric cooked me up some food using my opened package of pork. And it was a success! He also gave me some rice + beans—it was pretty delicious. He's done hiking in 2 days. I'm kind of disappointed because he's a real cool dude.

And story 2—Tangy has arrived! He showed up an hour or 2 ago. Not sure if I documented this, but we lost track of each other the past day and a half or so.

Tomorrow is going to be a long day—20 miles to Cosby Knob Shelter. This way, I only have 10 miles into Standing Bear Farm. So I can get in there early + relax. Tomorrow may be just a bit long. But should be worth it. Alright, I'm going to hit the hay.

One more story. When leaving camp this morning I was walking with that older woman. We were having a nice conversation when we started to incline a little. A bit brashly, she said, "I'm slowing down. Hike your own hike man!" It was a little awkward, so I didn't say anything + just left her behind. I saw her up at Clingman's Dome and we shared a greeting, but it was strange. I'm not sure if she was upset about being slower, or her injury (she has tendonitis issues like me), but it was a little off-putting. But either way, I wish her well. She went into Gatlinburg from Clingman's Dome today. I hope she makes it all the way—we shall see.

May 23 Notes: Cedric was sinewy and lean. He was in his mid twenties, but he looked older than that. His fair skin and scruffy goatee did not call to mind his native heritage. But on his face, he had several blue ink tattoos, visible marks of his native blood. He was an iron worker, and he looked like it. But behind that look was the quiet contemplation of an artist. He was a loner for the most part, preferring his tent's solitude to boisterous shelter chatter. I enjoyed his concrete presence: he did not have to speak in order for you to know he was there. Cedric was a section hiker, someone who plans on doing the entire trail in a series of sections, sometimes spanning many years. His small section finished up at I-40, just a mile short of Standing Bear Farm. I only knew him for about a week, but he is burned in my mind.

I met Jupiter at Ice Water for the first time. Jupiter was a veteran nearing thirty, his triangular face flanked on all sides by thin patches of hair and beard. Jupiter was Honorably Discharged from the Army after a parachuting injury. Depressed and confused, he began hiking the AT as a way to transition back into life as a civilian. He was a jubilant, quirky guy—odd and loving. Although I didn't know him for long, he was a quick friend, ready to listen to a story, and ready to pour his heart out. He too was a section hiker. He eventually left the trail in Virginia to take care of things at home.

Tangy arrived at Ice Water just a little bit after Cedric and I finished eating dinner. The skies were beginning to open up. Mists of cold swirled around us as night moved in. With my rain coat on, I stood at the opening to Tangy's tent, organizing our plan as we moved toward Hot Springs, North Carolina. If we lost each other, we would meet up on Max Patch in two days' time. I brushed my teeth and settled into my tent as the vapors of water turned to darts of rain.

I don't know what happened to the woman who told me to hike my own hike. I have since forgotten her name. I never saw her again.

May 24

Cosby Knob Shelter: 230.1

Today was a long day. I did about 20 miles, and my body feels that way. My right knee hurts a bit—which sucks. Luckily tomorrow is a short 10 mile day. So I'll have most of the day to rest.

This morning was crap + cold. Was about 45 degrees + raining when I woke up. It took a while to pack everything up because of that. I hit the trail with Cedric about 8am. It rained until about noon probably. I was pretty soaked, especially feet + lower legs. Luckily it stopped midday. We ate lunch at one of the shelters. Cedric made some refried beans he found at Newfound Gap. They were pretty good. The rest of the day was uneventful, but dreadful. Tons of terrible rocks—not big enough + not small enough for comfort. And lots of step down stairs. My knee does not enjoy that stuff + I feel it now.

I just hope it doesn't rain tonight. And I hope my knee is fine. I just want to get to Standing Bear + shower + have some beers. That is the plan.

May 24 Notes: Through the night at Ice Water Shelter and into the morning, the rain came down in cold darts, plunging into tents and shelters alike. I woke up in the grey and packed up my wet tent with hands that were stiff and numb. I didn't have gloves, so I wrapped my hands in bandanas, then put my second pair of socks over them. I poked my thumbs out of the holes that were worn through the heels, allowing me to hold onto my trekking poles. I hiked, and water began to soak through the nylon of my rain jacket, pooling in the depressions at my elbows.

Cedric and I left the other hikers, including Tangy, at the shelter. We were ready to get on with our day despite the weather. Before we headed out, Cedric told me he had to take a crap: *People say they don't like to take a crap when it's cold. But that doesn't make sense. Because your body needs to use extra energy to keep your shit warm, not your body. So I'm going to take a crap, then we'll go.*

Cedric was a hiker of the old school. His pack was an old army surplus pack, and his rain cover was a blue piece of tarpaulin. In his right hand, he carried a thick branch that he found in the woods. His clothing was just as simple, blue jeans and a cotton shirt. When it rained, he put on a denim jacket. He had gear that most others scoffed at—too heavy, too much cotton, too uncomfortable. Even so, I never saw a hiker look more content upon the trail. I hiked a lot with him this day, and he shared with me about his childhood: raised on his father's stories of Vikings and gods and his mother's stories of spirit and earth. His religion was a synthesis of those: a spirituality that defied label. He believed the world's major religions were blind cults following common men or dogmatic systems that held no truth. Yet he voiced his opinions in a manner that was neither disrespectful nor combative. He stated them as though they were timeless facts. He shared with me the struggles of being a white skinned Native American growing up on a reservation. He looked different than all of the other kids, and like all young children seeking a place, they let him know it. Cedric forced me to think about things beyond social labels and beyond the tangible aspects of our lives—both of creed and race. He forced me to think beyond the tangibility of life itself.

I lost Cedric for several hours after lunch. I became miserable. This was my first hike of twenty miles or more. The step downs did not match well with my gait. I felt my knees struggle with each lunge and drop. With a few miles left before Cosby Knob Shelter, I caught up to Cedric. *At least you know you can do a long day now,* he said. We hiked together into camp. He reminded me about something I had forgotten: I was a thru-hiker, and thru-hikers struggle.

May 25 + 26

Campsite: 254.6

So a lot has happened in the past day and a half, so I'll try to get it all down. There are a lot of events + thoughts I want to put down.

First off, my knee was a little twitchy last night, but it seems to be fine—normal aches.

Yesterday was probably the nicest day in the Smokies—as well as my last. Honestly, I'm not a big fan of the Smokies I don't think. Here are the reasons: —you need to pay to get in there (thanks federal gov't) —you need to go through a complicated process to get the permit —you need to (although I only did one night) sleep in packed shelters —there are barely any springs (only really at shelters) —the weather was crappy (not in anyone's control though) —and there are too many of those damn steps. They killed my knee the other day.

With that said, it was not terrible. I just wouldn't go back. However, there were some really nice views that I got to see yesterday. So that salvaged the Smokies a bit.

One of those views was pretty special. It wasn't much different than others, but it got me thinking about the land. I was high up so I could see really far—many gaps + mountains. I thought, "What if I own that land, even just a portion. Say from this ridge to this one." That got me thinking about what it means to "own" the land. We don't really own the land, even though we call it that, and many treat it as complete ownership. What we actually have with the land is stewardship over it. We should be there to care for it until it is passed to the next steward. Yes, we can—and should—reap benefits from it. But we can not destroy or disfigure it, it must be able to return to its natural state. The land is something special, it's part of the earth, and the place we live. It is much greater than us + will be here long after us. We can destroy it, but it will be remade. We are the Earth's Stewards—not its inhabitants.

Glad I got that on paper. I need to read more Thomas Berry books. I need to bring one of his books on this—I have no books. I have the time + brain power to read—so I need to.

So anyway, I finally left the Smokies yesterday. And I spent the second half of the day and night at Standing Bear Farm. I was chilling + drinking + eating starting at like 1 pm—it was great. Tangy, Jupiter, Raven, Rojo, some other dude + and a girl (forget their names) showed up around five. So we all hung out, drank, ate, etc.

I also did my first ever load of wash by hand at Standing Bear. This place was great. They had about 5 small buildings in the complex—bunkhouse, shower house, privy, kitchen, pantry, laundry room, and beer shack. It was great. The caretaker's name was Rocket. He's like a 65 year old former Marine + hippie. He literally just hangs out with people staying there. Crazy life.

So that was yesterday. Today I hiked about 14 miles and am now sitting on Max Patch. It's a nice bald with some great views. Tangy just arrived, so I'll write later.

Picking this up again at night. One thing I forgot about yesterday is that Cedric got off the trail at I-40. It was fun hiking with him. I learned that he's an Ossage Indian. I need to look them up. It would have been cool if he was going thru—but oh well.

So back to today. When I left off Tangy came up + we just chilled on the bald for a while. Then I came down to find our campsite about a half mile down. We ate, then went back to Max Patch to catch the sunset. It was great. Just got back a bit ago. Early in the morning we'll go back up to catch the sunrise—should be awesome. I got some great pictures already.

Anyway, it's 9:45 already. So time for bed. Got 20 to Hot Springs tomorrow, but it should be rocking!

I saw a bear my last day in the Smokies. Forgot to write that. Looked like a cub—I was about 70 ft away.

May 25 + 26 Notes: Standing Bear is an old tobacco farm that stands less than a mile off the trail. It's a collection of several small structures: more of a complex than anything else. It is simple, unapologetic, and odd. It has a reputation for being either loved or hated by those who stay there, as partying is a primary activity at this hostel. So it's easy to see how some folks would not be comfortable with the atmosphere. The caretaker, Rocket, cultivated the party atmosphere with little effort. He had a grizzly white beard and long white hair that flowed openly over his shoulders. In his hand was always a can of beer. When he was in sight, he moved quickly, but most of the time he was like a ghost, hidden somewhere in the Standing Bear complex. Between gulps of beer, he showed me each structure in the complex before unlocking the beer shack and handing me two beers. *Let me know if you need anything.* Then he left me to my own devices. I unpacked, showered, and washed my clothes. My beers went down quickly, and the beer shack, although locked, was quickly opened upon request. After completing my chores, Tangy and the other hikers showed up.

The girl I could not name in the above entry was short, with long brown hair covered by a trucker hat that seemed to never leave her head. Her name was Party, a fitting monicker given our location. She hung around a kid named Shaman, who was having a rough time on the trail and was dealing with some issues back home. They both tended to steer clear of me while at Standing Bear. I was suffering from allergies and I was snot rocketing everywhere. Everyone at Standing Bear stayed up late that night, eating frozen pizzas and candy bars and drinking beers. Rocket gave us a tour of his small shack: a one room structure that sat beside the shower house. We got more beers. We sat on the bunkhouse porch sharing trail stories. Got more beers. Then I woke up in my bunk in the morning. Standing Bear had lived up to its reputation as a trail-side oasis.

The next night, after hiking away from Standing Bear, Tangy and I made camp at the foot of Max Patch. As the sun began to dip, we climbed atop the open bald. The skies reddened. We took pictures, stealing the light through a lens. But our obligatory cameras mostly lay idle. The sun began to bleed orange and red, it leaked into the sky. The rolling hills held the darkness of the earth, sustaining shades of purple and brown. Dark below, light above. The collage of colors subtly changed hues, so that every moment seemed the same, but was different. We sat in silence as the flame died. It turned into a fine sliver as it sunk behind the last hill, and all that remained was its glow. We walked down to our campsite. I had seen the most beautiful sunset of my life.

May 29th

Spring Mountain Shelter: 284.9

The sunrise up on Max Patch was nice. Not as powerful as the sunset, but it was refreshing—a great way to start the day.

The hike was solid—we got a real early jump and knocked out the 20 miles by about 3pm. Me + Tangy picked up Jupiter around mid day and the three of us finished together.

Hot Springs... not as big as I thought it would be. It's really only one street with some bars, stores, houses on it. Cool town though. So we got in + went to Elmer's Sunnybrook Hostel—hands down my favorite place so far. It's an old Victorian home built around 1850 and renovated in 1875 or so. Really it's like a B+B for hikers. Hikers don't need to make reservations, but regular guests do. There are probably about 10 bedrooms. Then there's the kitchen, dining room, sitting room, music room all down stairs. Elmer + his crew (there were 2—Sticks + Matt—both cool guys) cook breakfast and dinner every day. It's only 6 bucks for breakfast + 10 for dinner. It's all vegetarian grub, but it's delicious!

Elmer is a unique man. He served in the first class of the Peace Corps, was a professor of Eastern Religions at Duke (I think), then hiked the trail. When he finished, he went to work at the hostel, and eventually wound up buying it.

The hostel has a very unique quality to it—he fosters community and personal relationships through it. He does this primarily through the meals. At each meal, everyone introduces themselves + says where they're from, their name, what they did before the trail, and what they hope to do after. It really is a neat experience.

I believe Elmer is a Buddhist. He has tons of books all over the house that you can read. I read about a quarter of a book called "Being Dharma." It was interesting—I plan to read it when I'm home. I never had much interaction with Buddhism, but it seems like a nice religion. I'd like to learn more about it. On top of all the books, the music room has a piano, guitars, banjos, some wind instruments, and some percussion. So it's a great place of learning, art, + music. It felt like an old aristocratic mansion that had fallen out of monetary favor, but still kept its spirit. It was neat.

Anyway, back to events. Me + Tangy split a room, dropped our stuff in, then went to the diner across the street. I got the Hungry Hiker. It's a big, really good burger. Delicious! Then we just did some errands then went to the bar to watch the Red Wings lose. I didn't do dinner at Elmer's—it was already full.

On my zero, I did a bunch more errands—resupply, computer, blog, etc. I ate scrambled eggs and grits at Elmer's. I updated my blog with Trail Update #3, then followed that a few hours later with my Trail Gremlins joke on Morgan. It got a good laugh (out of me at least!).

For lunch I crushed a salad + beer at the bar. And for dinner at Elmer's, we had a cauliflower soup, a garden salad, then the main dish of curried veggie stir fry with rice, followed by key lime pie for dessert. It was awesome! I went back for thirds I think. I couldn't stop eating.

At dinner, Elmer asked a question of us on top of the intros (dinner is me, Jupiter, Strider, Raven, Pockets, Shaman). He asked if you could witness one historical event, what would it be? I said the 1916 Easter Rising. Jupiter—first Tibetan self immolation. Sticks—Wright Bros Flight. Then some others said Moon landing, JFK assassination, I forget the rest. It was fun. We did a couple of other questions (what sound would you be? and another I forget). It was really fun + really neat. I enjoyed dinner greatly.

After dinner, we just hit the bar and hung out. Tangy was there with an Asheville friend, and 2 crazy girls were doing some weird stuff. It was kind of a weak night. I left at like midnight for some sleep.

So that brings me to today. I departed Elmer's with a heavy heart after eating waffles + strawberries for breakfast. Shaman + Rojo got shuttled to Asheville by Matt (Rojo for some interview + Shaman is leaving the trail—his mom is sick). Me + Tangy got to take stuff from Shaman's maildrop. It was great—got like 3 Clif Bars, 3 of those ProMeal bars, and like 3 or 4 other bar type things. Super awesome, but now I have a ton of food.

The hike to this shelter was only 12 miles, but I felt sluggish. My pack is heavy, and getting into it after a zero is tough. But I made it. Raven, Pockets, Jupiter, and Strider are here too. We're all hitting the hay pretty early. I'm actually going to start reading a Mitch Albom book I got for 75 cents at the Hot Springs Library. Can't beat that!

So the past couple of days were a blast. Elmer's was amazing, and I got to hang with some other thru hikers. So it sucks to leave it, but the trail calls! One step, one mile, one day at a time! Can't wait for Nashville!

May 29 Notes: I thought Hot Springs would be much bigger. Maybe some gridded streets, a strip mall or two, a bunch of bars and restaurants, maybe even a couple of hotels. But what I got was really just a single road, Bridge Street, down the middle of a small town. There I found a few bars and restaurants, a laundromat, some convenience stores, an outfitter, a library, Elmer's, some residential homes, and Spring Creek. Although it wasn't what I was expecting, it was exactly what I wanted.

Elmer's stands on a small rise, just off of Bridge Street, about a half mile before Spring Creek. Walking around to the back entrance, I got the feeling that the house was haunted, or would be haunted sometime in the near future. But as I entered through the back door and into the kitchen, I wondered if haunting a place like this wouldn't be too bad. The kitchen was large and full of wonderful Asian aromas. Elmer stood over a pan, his white hair and round glasses gave him the look of a professor. Elmer, along with Sticks and Matt, was busy at work cooking up the night's meal for a foraging club that was in town. After our quick welcome, Matt ushered us away from the kitchen to our room. We ascended the majestic staircase. I placed my pack down, careful not to disrupt the antique furniture as Matt scurried back downstairs to rejoin the cooking. I felt like a prodigal stooge returning to my old home.

Tangy and I stayed in a room perfumed with the spirit of the AT. Earl Shaffer, the first man to thru-hike the AT in 1948, stayed in that very room on two of his three thru-hikes. On the door of the room is a plaque commemorating Earl Shaffer and his thru-hikes of the Appalachian Trail. However, Elmer must not have paid too much attention to the words on the plaque when he had it made. If you look carefully, it says: "Earl Shaffer — Pioneer AT Thur-Hiker — Slept Here 1948 & 1998". Thru is spelled wrong in it. So according to the plaque, he's not a Thru-Hiker, he's a Thur(sday) Hiker! He only hikes on Thursdays. Tangy and I got a laugh out of it at least.

After a couple of nights at Elmer's, and with my health in order and my spirits high, leaving Hot Springs was difficult. I set out in the vicinity of several new friends, including Jupiter, Fiddlehead, Dream Catcher, Raven (aka Rylu), and Strider. As I left town, I ran into Munchies, who was just arriving in Hot Springs. He had caught me up after surviving the bed bug incident and his knee pain. The visor was dirtier and his beard slightly thicker. The trail experience had changed so much since that first day atop Springer Mountain with him. He was with a group of hikers I did not know, I was with a group of hikers he did not know. Less than a month into my hike, we were different. I missed the early days of the trail when it was just Sir Stooge, Tangy, and Munchies. Tangy was still back at Elmer's. He took a second zero in Hot Springs on the day that I departed. In six days, I would arrive in Erwin, Tennessee. From there, I would go to Nashville for the bachelor party of a hometown friend. Both Tangy and Munchies would continue north, passing me by during my seven days off the trail. Less than 300 miles into my thru-hike, I lost my first friends.

June 1 - Day 27 (I believe)

Whistling Gap: 328.6

I didn't write the past couple of days, but honestly not much has happened. I've been hiking mostly with Raven (he wants a new name because of that German girl ahead of us who is also called Raven) and Strider. I normally leave before they wake up, but we wind up in the same spots. I've also been hanging around this middle aged guy from Pittsburgh. He's just sectioning from Hot Springs to Erwin, so I'll lose him tomorrow. Nice guy though.

So leaving Hot Springs, Tangy stayed behind to watch Game 7 of the Red Wings. That's why I'm hanging with Strider + Raven.

On the trail, it's been pretty standard. I'm in no rush to Erwin since I don't need to be in Nashville until the fifth. I heard Erwin is terrible, so I may stay in Johnson City—need to do some research though. I'll figure that out tomorrow.

Anyway, the big news has to do with that damn Hoboken apartment. I turned my phone on last night just to check stuff out, and I have a voicemail from the landlord (never spoke to the guy in my life) and a text from the kid Chris who moved into my apartment. The voicemail said something about a leak and about how he didn't get rent (for April he did though) and Chris' text said the landlord contacted him and told him he shouldn't have given me the security deposit. Anyway, the landlord is an idiot—we paid him for April, and he got a third of May (from Chris). And this moron has been so hands off, he doesn't even know how transactions have been happening at the apartment. So Chris has kind of been a middleman because I'm not talking to the landlord—I'm done with this crap. I gave Chris the April payment info, and as far as the security deposit, oh well. If Dave the landlord wants to pony up $3150 for our deposits, I'll gladly return Chris' $1050. I'm just waiting it out for now. If Dave wants to know about how stuff worked, he can talk to Katie. And I'm not asking him for $3150 because he'll say no.

So I just gave Chris the April payment info and I'll wait it out until Erwin. I checked my phone today, and no new chatter, so whatever. I just want this stuff done with.

But anyway, yesterday was such a good day until I got those messages. I thought a lot about the Tree of Life and figured some more stuff out. I need to write it down tonight. I also thought some about what I want to do after this trip. I'm going to start a list. Short term though, I want to interview Nan + Pop, and Grandma about their lives. I wanted to do that with Gramp and never did. So I want to do it with them. I think I'll videotape + take notes, then put all the info into a book. I can also have them write up a part that won't be opened until they pass. It will be a nice way to have their life story.

The reason I started thinking about this is because I was thinking about death, and the Tree of Life. When we die, our bodies return to the Earth, our Soul to the One/God, but what about our minds? They stay with the other minds of the world, they stay with humanity + mankind. So it's our duty to record those minds before they are lost. That's why I want to interview Nan + Pop + Grandma. I'll write more about that later but my thinking later turned into this idea to record their stories.

So anyway, that's the past couple of days. Damn Hobo apartment crap is still lingering—all I want is for that to go away! But I know that doesn't really matter much—it's just some dumb stuff I need to deal with in the world.

June 1 Notes: The trail was such a release from the outside world. It was easy to get lost in the peace and community of long distance hiking. The voice message about my former apartment brought me back to the world outside the trail. I had to think about money, material obligations—things I cared about, but did not want to. I thought when I stepped foot on the AT that I would be free to think of what I wanted. With the voicemail, my idealism was dragged down in worry. I brooded on the issue and dreaded the confrontation that may arise from it. It turned out to not be too big of a deal. In Johnson City, I called the landlord and it was settled. I lost money, but at least I was free of the burden.

Strider and Rylu (aka Raven) looked like cousins—dark faces and dark eyes. But Strider's round face and deep set eyes always seemed to smile. Rylu's angular face and quiet demeanor seemed to hold something back. After reaching Erwin, I never saw Strider again. He was sectioning to Harper's Ferry and I never caught back up with him after my return. I would not see Rylu for months after Erwin. In Erwin, he would befriend a brother and sister and their trio would go by the name of Team Hustle and Flow. But for now he was Raven, or "the other Raven" as some people called him. His decision to change his name to Rylu came after discovering that a German girl, with the trail name of Raven, was hiking up ahead of him. Around Erwin he began going by Rylu, trying to set himself free of the German Raven's shadow.

I only hiked a few days with Rusty, the guy from Pittsburgh. He was a nice guy, a young dad and a kind, quiet man. He gave me a freeze dried meal when he left the trail from Erwin. He also found my blog several weeks after he returned home. He sent me an email wishing me luck on the rest of my trip. An image was attached to the email: a distant, yellow shirted stooge walking in the midst of the titanic Tennessee hills. The speck, despite its small stature amongst the hills, has the great gift of consciousness, a reminder of the power of that which can not be seen so easily: thought, creativity, and love.

6-10-13

Cherry Gap Shelter: 359.0

Holy cow—I'm behind. Reason being, not much happened prior to the bachelor party. Anyway, I spent one night, I believe last Sunday (?) at Uncle Johnny's in Erwin. Pretty cool place. It's right on the Nolichucky River. Pretty standard hiker hostel—bunk room (they did have some cabins though), bathroom/shower, and a small outfitter.

One thing that stood out big time about Uncle Johnny's was this really weird dude who was working/volunteering there. I learned some of his story on Monday when he drove me into Johnson City to the hotel. So this guy says he's a former intelligence operative of some sort who now lives in Mexico. He gave the air that he held some information that he was thinking about leaking. He kept saying he had a government car and the gov't was paying for him to be there, etc, etc. Anyway, it was all very cryptic + nebulous. Either he actually is/was a spook and knows what he's talking about (unlikely, in my thoughts) OR he is a delusional schizophrenic (more likely, in my estimation). Either way, nice guy, just really bizarre + strange. I really think he was a schizophrenic. He hiked back in the nineties, and said he was doing all this, volunteering and trail magic, to repay all the trail magic he got. So he said he's spent about 2k trail magicking people in the past month or two. Really nice guy, I just think his mind is not right.

So anyway, one night in Erwin, then two nights in Johnson City at a Red Roof. It was relaxing. I had a fridge in my room, so got cold cuts + cereal + milk and just crushed food, drank some beers, watched TV (lots of Cartoon Network), and read a lot (Anthem by Rand, and Einstein's Dreams).

So that was a good couple nights. Then I got the rental car Wednesday morning to head to Nashville. Drive there wasn't too bad—about 4 hours. I scooped Matt at the airport, and the bachelor party began. Me, Matt, Higgins, Celli, and Fagan were the Wednesday night crew. We went to this sweet steakhouse that night called Jimmy Kelly's. It was great. Got a nice little surf + turf. Then we just partied.

Then Thursday, Friday, Saturday were just constant party. My body was not up to the task. I partied, but I was hurting big time. It was a fun extended weekend though. Good to see everyone + party a bit. Only bad thing was Nashville was absolutely packed because of the Country Music Awards. But hey, it was a good time—can't complain.

So that was Nashville + Celli's bach party. It was a pretty wild, fun time. On Sunday, I drove back to Johnson

City, but didn't get to the Enterprise in time to drop the car off. So I had to get a hotel last night. Not bad. It was good starting in the morning as opposed to just doing a few miles. Now I'm at Cherry Gap Shelter I think. About 18 miles from Erwin. Frosty is here, and he gave me some rough news. The Neurovirus hit a bunch of people this past week. Party, Tangy, and a few others I don't know lost some days to the virus.

I felt kind of crappy on Friday in Nashville—I wonder if I had a very mild case. Frosty said some people got it real bad —one kid was hospitalized. I am kind of hoping my poo attacks a few days ago were it—maybe I'll get some nice immunity. I hope I don't get it!

So I need to figure out where Tangy is—he may not be too far ahead of me, maybe just a few days.

I just ate that bacon + egg Mountain House meal that Rusty magicked to me—it was good. I may get some of them every once in a while.

Frosty and this other guy here are making a fire now. I'll probably chill with them for a bit and then crash. Today was an early day.

I need to update the blog big time. I haven't updated since my trail gremlin joke. I may try to do some via my phone before I reach Damascus. There are also a couple hostels before Damascus I may hit. I need to do some big time research tonight to figure out my plans leading up to Mom + Dad's party. I shall update on that at a later time.

Mom + Dad finished their pilgrimage as well. They killed it. I can't believe they did as many miles as they did. Good job by them. I'm excited to see them in a few weeks for their party. I really need to haul in the weeks leading up to that so I'm in good shape getting to Harper's Ferry. More planning to do!

June 10 Notes: As I neared Uncle Johnny's hostel, I could hear the hum of the Nolichucky below me. The rains picked up and everything was grey through the trees. I reached the outpost on the river and dropped my pack under the awning of the outfitter. With Celli's bachelor party coming up, I was done hiking for seven days.

Rylu, Jupiter, Strider, Fiddlehead, and Dream Catcher all spent the night at Uncle Johnny's. Fiddlehead was a musically talented young woman—hence the trail name. She was bright, beautiful, and fun loving. She was friends with more people than I could even name on the trail. At Uncle Johnny's, I met one of her many friends by the name of Music Man. He was middle aged, a blue collar guy from somewhere in the northeast. He looked like a cartoon: bald head, scrunched face, and seemingly missing teeth—although I think they were all there. He was loud and brash, and he moved about violently. We struck up a conversation, as oftentimes happens, over the trail in general. He gave me his life story in short order, each detail landing like a punch. He spoke so quickly and about so many different things that I couldn't organize all the information.

What I did gather was that he was beginning to run short of money. He planned to hike up to Harper's Ferry, find a job there doing some construction work, save up some money, then continue on from there. I nodded and agreed with his comments and his plans, and before I knew it, Music Man was out of the bunkroom and our conversation was over. I thought I'd never see him again, but I wasn't sure how I felt about that. Behind the uneasiness, there was something that pulled me in. I felt like I was staring at a death fight. The violence seemed to hold some kind of truth.

The next morning, I was driven to Johnson City by the volunteer at Uncle Johnny's. During the twenty minute ride, the words that came out of this man's mouth scared and intrigued me. I've uncertainly come to the conclusion that he was a mentally ill individual. When he wasn't talking about charity work in Central and South America, or making questionable comments about some of the female hikers (he told me he was going to purchase underwear for one of them), he was telling me about world wide conspiracies. All of these conspiracies were being carried out by an American governmental organization, of which his cousin was the leader, and were massive in scope. One involved the use of devices to alter the physical landscape of the western US. He told me all this information without an ounce of uncertainty. We drove

47

toward Johnson City. Any threat of silence was quickly headed off by a new story or a new conspiracy. I never felt threatened by him directly. But he was trusting me too much with what he perceived to be valuable and powerful information, almost as if he were trying to pull me into whatever delusion he was experiencing. I nodded in agreement or acted shocked where necessary. He dropped me off at the hotel and we parted with a handshake. He was not a bad person, but I was glad to be free of the weight of his tortuous mind.

After a short break in Johnson City, I entered into the unbridled intensity of the bachelor party. Johnson City acted as a small buffer between the sublimity of the trail and the modern city life of Nashville, but it was not a large one. My body and mind were in shock as I spent several days drinking, eating, walking all over Nashville, and dancing like a stooge. In time, I began to long for the trail.

I drove from Nashville to Johnson City and spent the night there. In the morning, I was dropped off at Uncle Johnny's by the car rental company. I saw the delusional volunteer and we shared a quick hello before I started north across the Nolichucky River. The quiet of the woods took me in once again. It didn't ask where I had gone, or hinder my steps as I walked off of pavement and onto the soft, spongy ground. In a haze, I moved toward the misty beauty of the rolling Roan Highlands, seeing few people and few landmarks. A cloud of fog seemed to surround me at the top of each bald. It was as if I walked through the Underworld, making my way blindly toward some unknown destination. One foot came down upon the trail, then the next. It was easy to walk. My feet always fell toward earth. In the fog and mists of southern Virginia, I sought out the names of my friends in the shelter logs. I tracked their movements, hoping to catch them around the next bend or at the next shelter. Alongside Tangy's name, I began to see the name *Colonel Patches*. Colonel Patches was like the fog, something real but not fully tangible—more a spirit of progress than a real man. I knew nothing of him but his scraggly signature in the shelter logs, always several days ahead.

6-11-13

Roan High Knob Shelter: 375.8

Up on the highest shelter on the AT at High Roan. Today was pretty rough. I was burnt out for some reason. The climb up Roan Mountain was pretty tough. It was about an 18 mile day. Tomorrow is only about 14 though. I have my plan up to Damascus now. I should get there the 17th. That leaves me about 10 days before Mom + Dad's party. I should be able to cover good miles in those 10 days. I don't think I'll get to Harper's Ferry before July 15th (the unofficial cut off for reaching Katahdin), but I think I'll still have a shot at going thru to Katahdin and not flip flopping. We shall see.

Today was rough though. Not sure if it was high elevation or what. But I was out of it. It was hard to concentrate on much of anything. I was just laboring, mentally + physically today. I'm going to hit the hay early tonight though. I got a late jump this morning. It's already 8:15. I'm going to read then sleep. Later.

June 11 Notes: I was looking to reach Damascus, the quarter way point of the AT, on June 17. I had to be home June 27. It was my parents' 35th Anniversary party—I could not miss it. I also had a high school buddy's wedding to attend on June 28. But jumping on and off the trail was frustrating. I felt like I was missing out on being part of the flowing group of thru-hikers that formed the AT community. I wanted to see my family back home and be a part of these events, but home seemed so far away when I was on the trail. The trail was home.

I started my thru-hike a bit later than is recommended. Getting free of work and out on the trail took longer than planned. So I started in early May as opposed to the recommended start time of mid-April. My late start coupled with my taking extra days off the trail made it more difficult for me to finish by mid-October, the unofficial deadline for summiting Katahdin. In order to hit that deadline, it is recommended that thru-hikers reach Harper's Ferry by July 15. Although all of these abstract dates seemed so far away, I had to think about them. It would be disappointing if I didn't reach Katahdin going straight thru. If necessary, however, I would flip flop: hiking north until I nearly ran out of time to reach Katahdin, then traveling to Katahdin via modern transportation and hiking south to complete an official (albeit non-traditional) thru-hike of the AT. But a flip flop felt illegitimate. I wanted to hike thru. And although I welcomed a break from hiking and wanted desperately to see my family, it hurt to leave the trail. I was a thru-hiker, and thru-hikers hike.

6-12-13

Former Site of Apple House Shelter: 391.2

Planned on a 14 today, but went on to 16 to the site of a former shelter. Decent day, felt my best since my return to the trail. Hung out with a cool group of guys at camp. Three middle aged guys, an older fella, and two young boys (12 + 13). The three guys are all buddies and the others are father + sons. All nice guys.

The other highlight was I met this lunatic who the older gentleman calls the Pilgrim. Supposedly, this moron saw a documentary on the AT and just started hiking it. He's got a huge dilapidated rucksack with a bunch of random stuff (notably his Great Grandmother's violin). These guys were telling me stories about him since he's kind of been tagging along with them the past couple days. He seems like he has a few screws loose. He came puffing down the trail looking for water when he literally just walked past a spring. He borrowed some of mine and I don't even think he filled up his. I think he's just a mentally dumb man. The old guy was killing me with his stories. They told the Pilgrim that he's a hazard on the trail. Anyway, this may not be the last I see of the Pilgrim.

That's it—going to read then turn in. Farewell.

P.S. My socks stink terribly tonight.

June 12 Notes: The Pilgrim walked down the trail toward me, his rucksack hanging loosely from one shoulder, sweat beading on his gaunt face and soaking his short brown hair. He drank my water quickly, then carried on as if nothing had happened. I watched as the violin dragged over the trail, bouncing happily at his feet. That is the only interaction I had with the Pilgrim. I never saw him again.

From the older gentleman at the campsite that night, and from some other hikers along the trail, I gathered a number of stories about the Pilgrim: how he fell out of a tree while trying to hang his bear bag, how he boiled hot water directly above some sleeping hikers, how he wore woman's foam shoulder pads to keep his dilapidated rucksack from cutting into his flesh, how he dragged his great grandmother's antique violin behind him on a string, and how he never learned to treat his water. Through these stories, the Pilgrim became more than a person to me. He became a myth, a fantastic fool, a cosmic jokester. What knowledge had he that allowed him to live like this?

And then I heard another story. The Pilgrim made camp with some hikers at a shelter one night. A fire was made, and they all sat down to pass some time before sleep. The Pilgrim pulled out a small case, telling the others that he needed some medicine from his medicine chest. He drew out a vial and consumed the contents: one of an assortment of psychedelic drugs.

When I heard this story, the legend of the fantastic fool became too easy to explain: it was just drugs. He wasn't a piece of imagination come alive. He wasn't a muse in the guise of a stooge. He was just a drugged-up kid who was a danger to himself and others. But when I think about him, I still hold out hope that the Pilgrim was something much greater than that.

6-13-13
Moreland Gap Shelter: 410.5

Today was pretty wild. It was an amazing day—but trying + exhausting. My plan was to do 17 to a stream with a campsite. So I started the day amazingly—let me back up.

Those guys last night + this morning said they were going to the B+B for breakfast. I forewent, knowing I had a long day ahead. I passed up what is supposed to be a very good place. So I got on the trail a little after 7. After a few miles, I came across Elk River, where I had my first nude nature swim! It was great—a little chilly, but refreshing. And I got a bit cleaned up in there. Luckily no one was there to laugh at my tiny schmeckel.

After leaving there, the hike was easy. Then I came across my second awesome experience of the day—Isaac's Cemetery. This is just some cemetery right off the trail. It was great. I dropped my pack and hung out in there for a bit checking out the headstones. It was made up mostly of generations of the same families—Jones, Potter, Isaac, Johnson, and a few others. There were new graves, and old. Some stretched back to the mid to late 1800's. There were even several "unknown" headstones. It was really a neat place —I'm glad I spent some time there.

After leaving the cemetery, all went well until mile 14. I was taking a breather when I heard thunder, then the skies darkened. I had only three miles to my proposed campsite (mile 17), so I decided to go for it. After a half mile, the skies opened up and I was caught smack in the middle of the storm. The lightning to thunder delay was amazing—like 3 or 4 seconds. The rain was torrential. The trail turned into a stream. I took refuge under a rock shelf to see if I could wait it out— no luck. So I braved the trek to my proposed campsite in the downpour. I was soaked to the muscles. I think my pockets were actually filling with water. I gave up on my clothes or body staying dry—I just hoped my pack would be fine.

I reached my stream campsite, but it was still pouring, so

I decided to push the two miles to the next shelter. Longest two miles ever. The rain finally slackened about a mile from the shelter, but the damage was done. Clothes soaked, pack a little wet, but nothing disastrous.

I found Party, and Tangy's two buddies at the shelter (I forget their names). So it was good to catch them. They pushed on 6 more miles to the hostel. I'm going to wake early and go there for some food + internet. So that was my day. Exciting + fun, and trying. But I'd say one of my favorite days yet. Excited for tomorrow!

June 13 Notes: At Elk River, I happily stripped down and entered the chilly, shallow waters. I spent ten minutes floating in the cold river. I submerged my body, wiping the days of dirt and sweat from me. I walked naked from the waters. The beads of water dried in the hot sun. I shooed flies away from my clothes and pulled the dirty rags back on. But I still felt clean.

At Moreland Gap Shelter I saw Party. She had a companion, a dog named EZ. He was a small Jack Russell Terrier with the agility and energy of a madman. Dogs are not allowed through the Smokies, so when I first met Party, EZ was in a kennel waiting to be picked up. With Party and EZ were Jason and Pete, the two guys who I could not recall in my entry. I had been briefly introduced to them by Tangy in Hot Springs. Jason was a big, strong guy with a dark, bushy beard. He laughed easily and enjoyed breaking logs for the fire. Pete, in his glasses and closely shorn beard, looked like an odd companion to Jason. His round face and pleasant grin were out of place with the harshness of Jason's log breaking way of life. Pete was easy going, but unlike Jason, he sometimes appeared more comfortable in his tent than in the open. Although I didn't know them well, I was glad to see three familiar faces when I reached the shelter. Party, Jason, and Pete pushed on to Black Bear Hostel that night. I holed up in my tent, exhausted from the battle through the storm.

6-14-13

Decent day today. Did about 14 or 16—I forget. We went up + over some pretty big mountain. Then down to a sweet lake, where I swam + hung for a few hours. Me, Party, Jason, + Pete were all hanging.

Earlier today, I woke super early so I could get to the Black Bear Hostel. I did laundry (all my clothes were soaked), showered, and had breakfast (2 frozen french bread pizzas), had coffee, drank one beer, then left. It was a nice little break. I got there a little after 8. So I actually woke up at 5 I think.

So the hostel was cool, then we went down to Laurel Falls. It was a super wide water fall. I was thinking of swimming, but I knew the lake was coming up.

Pretty uneventful day. I do have two blister issues—I think from the extreme wetness. The one on my right is fine. But my one on the left—I can't see an actual blister. It's like my callus just hurts. We'll see what tomorrow brings.

June 14 Notes: I woke in the darkness and turned on my headlamp. The searing whiteness lit up the tent. Above me, my still wet garments hung from lines that criss crossed the tent. It smelled like rain. I quickly pulled on my damp, cold underwear. I pulled on my pants. I couldn't muster the courage to pull on my wet shirt. I put on the only dry top garment I had—my down jacket. Hiking into the darkness, I set out toward Black Bear Hostel. The sun had not yet risen. Around this time, rain became a daily visitor. I learned to get through it as though it were a tedious daily chore, like setting up camp or cooking dinner. It rained almost daily until Harper's Ferry, 600 miles north.

After my morning at Black Bear Hostel, I hiked toward the lake at Shook Branch Recreation Area. I reached the lake thirty minutes before Party, Jason, and Pete, so I sat down on the warm grass and leaned against my pack. I pulled my worn shoes from my feet and the dirtied tape from my toes: blister treatments that got replaced daily. I pulled off my hiking pants and put on my shorts. As I walked toward the water's edge, I could tell I was the only hiker there. There were many families, and I hoped they would forgive me for using the lake as a bathing opportunity. The water was cool and refreshing. I climbed out and dried in the hot sun. Party, Jason, and Pete arrived. We received some trail magic—pizza, chips, and hot dogs. We ate everything the families were willing to give us. As we finished our first dinner of the night, we watched the sun drop slowly in the sky. To be in the open space of the beach was a refreshing break from the shady green tunnel of the trail. Before the sun dropped too far, we picked up our gear and left the beach, heading back into the tunnel to reach our campsite at the far side of the lake.

6-15-13

Campsite: 444.0

Nothing much went on today. Got a real late jump—left around 9. So my day was long. I only did about 16 miles, but I finished around 5:30.

I'm only about 24 miles or so from Damascus. Tomorrow I will probably do about 19, then wake early the next day and do the last 5 or so and have the whole day in town.

One awesome thing I forgot to mention yesterday. I used my tomahawk in the most awesome way. So far, I've just made a few walking staffs and hammered in my tent stakes. But yesterday, as I was climbing a mountain, I came across a big, freshly fallen tree. Right across the trail. It was a full tree, so you couldn't really go through it, nor around it on either side. So I busted out my tomahawk and started lopping off all the limbs around the trunk. It took about 10 minutes, and success. The main trunk was still there, but you could just hop over that easily. It was pretty awesome. Pete has a picture of it that I need to get from him.

Anyway, not much to write about today. Pretty low key. It's a little after 8, and I am probably going to turn in soon. Later!

June 15 Notes: Just before Shook Branch Recreation Area, I climbed over a 3,700 foot, nameless crest. As I walked along the switchbacks, evidence of the torrential storm of the previous day was everywhere. Freshly fallen trees lay on their sides, green leaves were scattered about, branches were ripped apart, and dried rivulets cut through the trail.

I approached the fallen tree, about twenty feet tall. Its bright green leaves were still intact upon the reaching branches. Tightening my pack against my body, I began to climb through the fallen foliage, battling with the gauntlet of grasping branches. They clung to my legs and arms, and jammed their way into the crevices of my pack. Defeated, I backed out to reassess the situation, and it was then that I remembered Party was behind me with EZ. With heroism rising in my gut, I dropped my pack to the bank of earth, unsheathed my tomahawk, lifted it to the sky, and drove it into the yielding arms of the fallen tree. My tomahawk finally had some questionably legitimate use.

6-21-13

Crawfish Trail: 548.5

Haven't written in a bit, so let's go through everything. Made a big push into Damascus (24 miles) instead of breaking it into 2 days. It was worth it since I then was able to take a zero in Damascus. The zero was necessary as I spent most of the day doing chores.

I hung out with Pete, Jason, Party, Wash, + Boo Bear. The night we got in we just chilled, went to the bar. It was a Sunday night, so that's all that was open. I stayed at 'The Place.' It was cool there. The caretaker, Atlas, is a character. Nice guy, big talker. Pete stayed there too. The others were scattered about.

On my zero, I did all my chores, updated my blog, etc. Then we hung at the bar. I got a pizza—delish!

Pete got off the trail at Damascus—he's done. He said he was just tired of it—he wants to do something else. So his friend picked him up + they're going golfing for a week or so, then he'll get back to the real world. Oh well.

Tuesday morning me, Party, Party's friend (she drove from Oregon to hike a week with Party), Pete, + Jason had breakfast. Then I hit the trail. I haven't seen any of them since.

One thing I forgot about Monday night—hilarious. So for dinner, we were going to go to 'Hey Joe's,' this Mexican place. Me + Pete head over there first since the others weren't ready. We get there, and a sign says 'Closed Mondays,' but you can blatantly hear people partying in there! So whatever, we go to the bar instead. While we're there, Party texts Pete + tells us to go to Hey Joe's because they got in. So we finish our beers + head there. It is hilarious. These three moron brothers own this restaurant. And they had recently finished a round of golf. So they're just hanging + partying with their friend who didn't say a word the whole time. So we just hang out, drink two dollar beers, eat a burrito, and listen to these idiots banter + play some music (they actually weren't too bad at that). So after an hour or two there, they invited us to keep partying at their house. I declined + went to the bar with some other hikers. The rest went to their house + said it was terrible. So it was a weird but funny time—hanging out with those idiots in a closed Mexican place.

So that was Damascus. Not a bad town—just not as cool as I thought it would be.

So I left Damascus Tuesday. Today is now Friday. Tuesday's weather was terrible. I got rained on most of the day. I hiked with Greenland, this dude I met at 'The Place' for Tuesday + Wednesday. He's a South Korean guy who's lived in NYC + Atlanta. Super funny + asian—really nice guy. I got a hilarious picture with him too. I also saw Conundrum for the first time in about a month. That was cool. Right now, I'm a ways out in front of them in my dash to reach Pearisburg so I can get home for Mom + Dad's party though. So hopefully I see them when I get back on.

Anyway, Tuesday I was soaked. That resulted in some blister issues on Wednesday. On Thursday, I decided to experiment with my shoes still wet + hurting—I went sockless in order to dry out quicker. It worked, I just got some blood spots on my feet though. So today they're a bit banged up—but recovering.

Yesterday's adventure also has something to do with my blood spots. I did my longest day yet—about 29 miles. I had planned about 20. But then I found out you can order pizza from Partnership Shelter which was 29 miles from me at the time. So I did it. That's how I left Conundrum, Greenland, Boo Bear, + Wash back a ways. It was worth it though. I met up with Eyes + we got the pizzas. Large pepperoni + it was awesome. I ate all but 2 slices, which I ate for breakfast this morning. Eyes is a cool dude. He started May 8th, and somehow yesterday was the first time I met him. Crazy.

So that brings me to today. Currently, I'm not exactly sure where I am. I did about 18 I think—but the guidebook is a little weird around here for some reason. I had lunch at 'The Barn' in Atkins VA today. I got a Hiker burger which was awesome. So last night I had pizza + today a burger—can't beat that.

Tomorrow should be a pretty tough day. I plan on doing around 20, but there are a lot of ascents + descents. So we'll see. The 2 days following that are real easy though. So not a big deal if I don't hit my 20 mark tomorrow.

Well I'm glad I got all this down now. The past few days have been long + tiring. But only a few more, then home for the party! Can't wait!!

Headed to bed now—night.

June 21 Notes: I began to slack on the frequency of journal entries. The reasons for this are numerous. For one, at the start of the trail, I conscientiously kept the practice of writing and recording my journey at the front of my mind. I made it a point to write as frequently as I could, whether it was about the trail or anything else. As I got deeper into my journey, the gritty details of my daily hike became more important: how many miles to go, where to sleep, where to get water. Those more basic thoughts pushed out my more elevated will to write. Secondly, the level of physical exertion began to increase drastically. At the start of the trail, I did about ten to fifteen miles per day. I would make camp in the early to mid afternoon and have time to do things. Aside from setting up camp and cooking, I would write, read, meet people, and peruse the campground. Once I began to put in more miles per day, I was more fatigued and had less time in camp. I would set up my tent and sleep system, retrieve water, cook, tend to any gear issues or medical needs, and then go to sleep. When I did take out my journal, I often couldn't finish the entry—I was just too tired. Lastly, it was now difficult to find time alone. The trail community was an intricate web of people and names. If I didn't know someone directly, I knew them through a friend. Being immersed in an expanding relationship network takes up a lot of time. I wish I had spent more time writing and recording my journey. It is a regret of mine that I lost some of my will to write. I wish I could recall every thought, every fleeting feeling I had by looking at a piece of paper, but I can not. Even so, I am content with what I do have. The fatigue was too overwhelming sometimes, I couldn't control it. I needed the rest when I needed it. And the times I spent with my many friends were invaluable. Although it may be difficult to recall some details of those times, I know that those interactions are still an integral part of who I am.

In Damascus, I was ready to see a thru-hiker paradise. I expected a bustling little town, ready to accept every downtrodden hiker that stumbled out of the woods and into the mecca of Trail Days. What I found instead was a Damascus that stood like forgotten hollowed ground of the Appalachian Trail. It was a forgettable town that seemed to lack something vital. Perhaps it was the fact that Trail Days had exhausted the population a couple of weeks before. I don't know. I can't recall too much of it now—just some stores, some homes, a Post Office, and a couple of restaurants. What I can recall vividly, however, is the hikers I met.

I first met Boo Bear and Wash about two miles before Damascus, at the TN/VA border. They spoke with a lilting drawl. To my northern ear, I couldn't pick out a state, they just sounded like southerners. Wash, the younger brother, was my age. He was intelligently horrifying, like an insane social scientist. I got the feeling he was conducting small social experiments at all times, reading and recording the reactions of others in his mind. The experiments always occurred with an ambiguously idiotic grin upon his face. Boo Bear was a couple of years older. He was tall, thin, and dark. He was just as big of a stooge as Wash and he played the part of the older brother well—not dominant or demeaning. He was a good person and a good brother. I felt it in his subtle show of protection and friendship with his brother, which Wash readily reciprocated.

On my zero in Damascus, I spotted a girl speaking with another hiker at the picnic area. She was beautiful. Her blonde ponytail hung straight to her shoulders, and she beamed a smile across her cherub face. She told me she was a hotshot. I was slightly taken aback by her audacity. I must have missed something, but I just pretended like I knew what a hotshot was. I later found out that she was a wildfire firefighter in a unit called the Interagency Hotshot Crew (hence the trail name Hotshot). She left Damascus a day before me. And despite my attempts to catch her, I saw her infrequently after Damascus. Although she was perhaps the best hiker I knew, I sometimes convinced her to slow down and hang around.

I met Greenland at The Place as I was unpacking my gear upon arrival. I first overheard him, in his heavy Asian accent, asking Atlas if there were any restaurants in town that served rice. *Rice? No. Not that I know of.* Greenland thanked him, smiled, and dug into his food bag instead. He was not disappointed or angry, he was content simply to have something to eat. I never met anyone quite like Greenland on the trail. He was like a caring father. At one shelter during lunch time, he patiently helped a young hiker cook Ramen over a camp stove. He never showed frustration at the simplicity of the task. He stood by the young man the whole time, telling him how to turn up the flame, when to put in the noodles, when to stir, when to season, and when to eat. The trail seemed too harsh of a place for such a gentle person. He was a close hiking companion of mine for about a week after leaving

Damascus. During that time, I enjoyed his fatherly presence, although we rarely shared a long conversation. In all honesty, his real trail name may have not been Greenland. Through his heavy accent, I never pinned down exactly what he was saying to me. Whatever his name might have been, he was a great friend. He left the trail in Roanoke, Virginia, about a week north of Damascus.

All of these people, and all those I did not mention, whether I knew them for a few days or a few months—or if I will continue to know them for years to come—have had an impact on me. Like the notes of a symphony, each interaction, word, or moment of silence has its place in my life. Without those notes, the symphony would be incomplete, broken, unfulfilled. It would not be the one that is written. They are integral pieces of the work. They are the booms of brass, the hum of strings, and the subtle spans of silence that lie between. Those notes make the symphony whole, and because they have been played, they are immortalized. They are eternal, forever bound to the music of life.

6-23-13

Campsite: 591.0

I'm exhausted. Pulled another 2 long days yesterday + today. Yesterday I was hurting towards the end of the day. But not a bad day hiking. I went to that old schoolhouse. I met a guy who thru hiked a few years ago—Director. Nice dude. He gave me some snacks and a gatorade. Nope—now I'm mixing up days. That was 2 days ago right before Atkins.

Yesterday at lunch I took a bath in a nice little creek, then had lunch while I dried. It was great until the bugs started going crazy. The rest of the day was standard—did almost 20.

Today I did about 22. Saw few people. Tomorrow is about another 20 then 2 easy days.

Last night I had the mac + cheese that Pete suggested. It was delicious. I'm definitely doing it again.

Well I'm a little achy + tired, so I'm going to turn in. Excited for tomorrow to be done. Then just 10 miles to Woods Hole Hostel, then 10 Wednesday morning into Pearisburg, then home!

June 23 Notes: Just before Atkins, Virginia is an old schoolhouse called the Lindamood School. The one room structure sits just off the trail in a small field. Everything about the place and its surroundings seems small. I walked up tiny stairs to get to the tiny building, and when I entered the schoolhouse, I saw small desks and a small chalkboard in the small room. On the walls hung replicas of small, old school posters. On one of the miniaturized desks, I saw something packaged in clear plastic: the perfection of the workings of the trail. Several days prior, my original utensil, a plastic camping spoon, had broken in half. It weakened down the middle from scraping burnt dinners out of the bottom of my cooking vessel. My attempts to repair the spoon had failed—the zip tie and safety pin splint lasted only a minute, and so, I was forced to eat my dinners with a two inch utensil. But what I saw in the clear packaging was too perfect to be a coincidence. An unknown Trail Angel had left a small packet of items for me. It contained some powdered creamer, a mixing stick, a napkin, and a cheap plastic spoon—the perfect temporary replacement. I slipped the magic into my pocket, turned to look at the smallness of the place once more, and walked outside.

A man walked up and asked if I was thru-hiking. *Yes*, I told him. *Ok, give me a minute, I have some things for you.* I drank the Gatorade he handed me and we talked. Director told me the story of when he came to the Lindamood School on his thru-hike. It was raining hard when he reached the schoolhouse, so he sought shelter inside. For several hours, he rode out the storm with five other hikers in that little place. He stared up at the structure, recalling the music of his thru-hike as he became a part of my own. With a shake of my hand, he wished me luck and turned back to his car. I spent the next ten minutes alone, except for the butterfly that flitted upon my hand, his brilliant blue wings catching the dry rays of the sun.

6-24-13

Dismal Creek: 611.0

Talk about good timing! So today was my last longer day before my 2 easy ones (10 to hostel, then 10 to Pearisburg). I left camp about 4 am this morning just because I felt like it. Got to my location today around 1 pm, so it was nice and early. I had a quick tuna burrito, then the skies got dark and opened up around 1:30. Luckily I had a few minutes to set up my tent. So for the first time in a storm during the day, I didn't get soaked. Now I'm just riding it out in my tent.

Today's hike was a little rough, mentally. The last few miles felt so long. It was hot and the bugs were brutal. Those stupid little gnats just don't leave you alone. But it's good now.

The storm has slowed a little. I'm going to do some reading.

June 24 Notes: I had finally been spared the rain. My tent went up as the first drops started to come down. I was safely within the taught barrier by the time the storm swept through. After writing this entry, I attempted to read. My tiredness got the best of me however, and I quickly dozed off to the sound of rain drops bombarding my tent.

I woke up a short time after. The smell of moist earth rose to my nostrils as I saw another hiker, soaking wet, hike past. I surveyed my camp with fresh eyes. I felt I was in my own little paradise. Beside my tent stood the short sloping shore to the stream. Above me, the trees hung loosely, soothing the swelling waters. I walked into the current and washed the dirt from my arms and face as the sun struggled to peek through the thinning clouds.

6-25-13

Woods Hole Hostel: 620.4

So I made it to Woods Hole Hostel—only 10 more to town. Just emailed Dad and the car rental is all ready to go.

Had two issues on today's short hike—but oh well, nothing major. First, I lost my white bandana. It must have fallen out of my pocket somewhere. And second, my water bladder sprung a leak. Nothing major, but you know.

Yesterday's camp was awesome. I was right on a creek, and it was just me. It may have been my favorite camp spot so far. This morning I took it easy at camp. Cooked some grits, then some coffee (from Boo Bear + Wash) and ate pop tarts.

Yesterday afternoon + today has been the first time in a while I didn't feel rushed. I need to focus more on that—just slowing down + enjoying.

Woods Hole hostel is alright. I planned on buying lunch here. But the guidebook lied. They don't have food to buy wherever, just some sodas + some candy bars. So I made some Ramen, ate a candy bar + some tuna. Tonight though, I'm having dinner that they cook. So I'm super pumped for that! Should be awesome. Then home tomorrow for more good food!

One last thing. Last night I did some surgery on my blister issue on my right foot, on the front pad. I thought I had fixed it a few days earlier, but no. As I was looking at it yesterday, it was like I had 2 malformed calluses on top of each other. No blister—there was no fluid. It was just like two fleshy, soggy calluses. So I just cut both of them off as much as I could. I think it helped as I don't have much pain today, nor did I while hiking earlier. So hopefully it just heals up and is good to go now!

I'll let you know how dinner goes. So dinner was pretty awesome. We helped make it. Patches + Hotshot were here, and one other girl, I missed her name. I cut up some chorizo + some pepperoni that they make here. The pizzas we made with them were delicious. There were peppers, tomatoes, onions, the pepperoni + chorizo, pesto + tomato sauce. They were all awesome. I ate a ton.

Then after dinner, we meditated for 30 min. I did pretty well. Only the last five minutes I struggled. I shouldn't have sat the way I was. My knees + hips felt it. And my left foot started to go numb. But I did pretty well. It was nice. People are all getting ready for bed, so it'll be lights out soon. Then an early, 10 mile hike, then home. Smell ya's later.

June 25 Notes: Woods Hole Hostel stands a mile off the AT down a wood lined dirt road. As I passed through the gates of the complex, the log cabin bunkhouse stood before me, weathered and welcoming. The red roofed farmhouse and the large garden rose up on my right, and the large, open pasture stretched out on my left. Goats milled about the rocks and grass, watching my approach through the wire fencing. I went inside to meet Neville, the owner. After a bustling reception and some quick instructions, I headed out to the bunkhouse. Climbing the ladder to the second floor of the bunkhouse, I saw Caribou, a young, spacey kid with shaggy hair. He looked at me like I wasn't there before returning to his sketch pad. As I unloaded my pack, I had a strange conversation with him before retreating back down the ladder. I showered off, cooked lunch, and waited for Patches to come through the gates of Woods Hole.

Patches was an intelligent New Englander with a flare for the outdoors. Her curly hair and wide, eager eyes matched the quirky broadness of her smile. Clipped to her pack was a banner that sported patches of trails she had hiked, some twenty or so in all—thus earning her the name Patches. I first met her a week earlier. She approached me, hiking south, a slack pack on, her poles working loosely and confidently. At first, we spoke briefly about nothing in particular—about water or the weather. She asked me my name. *Sir Stooge. And you?* She bounced in her shoes and mentioned Tangy's name. *I'm Patches.* I was puzzled. *So you're Patches!?* This was the ghost I had been looking for, the infamous Colonel Patches with the scratchy handwriting? The one I had imagined as a ghost, riding the wisps of fog through the Roan Highlands? *Oh, no. That's another*

Patches. That's not me. She went on to say that she was not Colonel Patches, but just Patches. Colonel Patches was a young kid with blonde hair. I felt somehow relieved that I hadn't found Colonel Patches yet. The timing, or the place, or the person didn't feel right. So although my hunt for the wraith named Colonel Patches continued, I gained a new friend. From that point on, Patches would become a frequent companion on the trail. As we advanced northward, she never seemed too far from me. She was always there to count on, to meet up with, and to enjoy the experience of the trail.

Several hours later, as Patches, Caribou, and I prepared the pizzas in the kitchen of the farmhouse, Hotshot came through the gates. Somehow and somewhere, I had passed by the best hiker I knew. We all shared laughs and stories as we cooked dinner with Neville. We chopped pepperoni and vegetables. We slathered pesto and tomato sauce onto Neville's home made pizza crust. And then we ate it all, quickly and happily, at a table full of friends.

The next morning, I woke at 4am. I slipped Hotshot a note with my phone number in the hopes that I would be able to catch her upon my return. With a heavy heart and a bag of mission figs from the hiker box, I hiked the ten miles into Pearisburg, Virginia, once again leaving behind my friends. My next destination was home.

7-3-13

Pickle Branch Shelter: 691.1

Obviously haven't written in a while. This is my third day back on the trail. Let me recount the past 3 hiking days before talking about my trip off the trail. It will be pretty short.

The theme has been rain. I started hiking Monday at about 11:30am after dropping the rental off. I left Mt. Laurel about 3:30am. Monday's hike was decent. Did about 20 to the Captain's and finished around 7:30. The Captain's was cool. It's just some guy's backyard, and he lets hikers sleep out there.

I was the only one there, so I just played with his two really cool dogs. Party (who I ran into about a mile into my day) was supposed to get to the Captain's, but never showed. She is moving so slowly, she's never going to make Katahdin in time. I haven't seen her since Monday. No rain Monday.

Tuesday + Wednesday, not much to say. It's been pretty miserable. Just lots of rain. My initial plan to reach Daleville tomorrow has been canned. Matt is instead going to pick me up at VA 311 tomorrow morning. We'll spend the 4th in town, hopefully catch some fireworks, then we'll hike about 45 miles where Matt will get shuttled back to his car on Sunday. So I'm excited for tomorrow—I'll get to dry my stuff out.

So back to my time off the trail—it was a blast. I got home Wednesday night around 7pm. It was good to be home. Then Thursday was a chill party prep day. And finally Friday was Mom + Dad's party! It was a blast. Everything went so well. Siblings did a great job with all the gifts. Uncle Jack spoke, Pop did 'Casey at the Bat,' and we all did Old King Cole. Then Dad hilariously sung "500 Miles" with the band playing. It was all just awesome. Lots of dancing, hanging, and having fun. Mom + Dad were so happy. It was great. It was really a special night, and I'm so glad I was a part of all of it.

That brings me to Saturday night, which was Dan + Nat's wedding night. It was really beautiful. I botched it and went a little late because I misread the invite so I missed the ceremony. But I made the cocktail hour + reception + all. It really was a nice, elegant wedding. Nat looked beautiful. Everyone was happy.

It was awesome seeing Leah + Gil + Liv too. And Mr. + Mrs. Johnson. And Brandon. I miss them. And I realized I really miss Leah. Anyway, turns out I had too much, Mr. Johnson got me a ride back home, and I left my jacket at the wedding. So the next morning I texted Leah to see if she had my jacket. Turns out Dan took it so I went to get it at the hotel he was at. Got in a fender bender—terrible. But I got my jacket. Then went to the farm to get my car. Leah told me to come by, so I did. It was good to be there again. I saw Liv + Mrs. J + Leah. I think I still love Leah. At the wedding, I think Nat told me I could probably get back with her. I think I'd like that. I've been thinking about her a lot the past few days.

Anyway, time for bed. It's pouring now. I really hope it isn't raining when I head out in the morning. That would be nice.

July 3 Notes: The world of the trail and the world of home were so different from each other. It was difficult to transition from one to the other, both in mind and body. One had toilets, the other had cat holes. One had electricity, the other had man power. One had neighborhoods, the other had the wilds. While at home, I still felt like a hiker. I woke from dreams and felt for my tent above me. My days of rest were underlined by a frustrated urge to move, and the flow of people in public felt like a collapsing wave. Despite the difficulties in transition, being at home gave me a perspective on the riches that I have there. My parents, who were celebrating their 35th Anniversary and their completion of a 200 mile section of the Camino in Spain, have always been my greatest support structure. My brothers and sister are my best friends. And all my other friends and family are integral pieces of my life. At the wedding, I saw a lot of old friends. I saw a girl who I have loved for many years. My return gave me a heightened perspective on what they all mean to me. But the trail still called my name, both in dreams and in waking. So I said my early morning goodbyes, drove through the night, and slid back into the woods.

Although I was surprised to see Party only a mile out of Pearisburg, I was happy to have a friend close by. Party explained that she, Tangy, and Jason had spent several zeros in Pearisburg. Then she dropped some sad news: while Party continued north, Jason and Tangy left the trail indefinitely, tired of the rain and drudgery of long distance hiking. One of my best friends was off the trail. The struggle of the Appalachian Trail seemed to be getting to all of us but EZ. He flopped, rolled, and scurried about my feet without a care. After planning to meet at The Captain's that night, I left Party and her companion behind. I struggled through the day as I found my trail legs once again. I was fatigued, both mentally and physically as I approached the Captain's. The sign for the Captain's pointed down a short bank to a pulley system that hung suspended over a stream. I sat on the plank of wood that served as a seat, grabbed hold of the lines strung out above me, and pulled myself across. It was an interesting mode of transportation, one that seemed quite sketchy considering the foot of water that flowed just below me. I made it across safely, set up my tent, and relaxed as the sun began to set. Party never showed. I spent the night at the Captain's with the two sheep dogs instead.

With Party slightly behind me, Tangy indefinitely off the trail, and the rest of my friends days ahead, the rain continued to be my most dependable companion. In the previous two weeks, the precipitation was a challenge. But now the constancy was becoming psychologically destructive. The sun did not appear. The trail was wet and puddled. My clothes and shoes no longer dried overnight, and my mind became fogged over. But still I could not hate the rain—it was too benevolent to despise. The drops soaked into the earth below me. They were refilling the springs that I drank from. The rain fell because it was supposed to, and I could do nothing but accept it.

The next morning, I arrived at a parking lot on VA-311 as the storm clouds gathered.

7-5-13

Campsite: 726.5

Matt's first day—he killed it. We did 23 miles! Ate dinner in town at a bbq joint, then hiked 3 miles out to a campsite. Matt did real well. One blister and a little sore—not bad at all for a long haul day. Enough said—awesome day. And a 19 tomorrow! See ya!

July 5 Notes: I waited for my brother Matt in a parking lot off of VA-311. I stripped off my clothes, freshly soaked from a rainstorm that morning, and laid them out on a rock to dry. The clouds darkened again and I strung up my rain fly across a couple of trees, hoping to stay relatively dry if the skies opened up. I heard a car pull into the lot: The Googan had arrived. Matt took his moniker from the derogatory name that legitimate fishermen use to describe rogue or illegitimate fishermen. But instead of Matt being a fisherman, he was a weekend hiker without a clue—a googan. Despite his self-degrading name, he did a noble job of hiking. Along with his machete and heavy tent, Matt brought some sunshine with him. In the two and a half days he was with me, we didn't get a drop of rain. He stepped out of his car, broad shouldered, scruffy, and confident. His excitement for hiking was evident, but he would have to wait one more day to hit the trail. The day of his arrival, the Fourth of July, we spent in town. On the fifth, we started at VA-311 and hiked 20 miles north. We found ourselves at a barbecue restaurant in Daleville. So we stuffed our faces with food and beer, thinking we could make camp less than a mile north. Unfortunately, there were several easements as we left town, pushing us about three miles up the trail. As we trudged our last leg of the journey, searching for any flat ground upon which to make camp, I heard behind me, *Dude, what do we do if we don't find a campsite?* The Googan assumed possible death if we couldn't find a campsite anytime soon, and in his fatigue and discomfort, he sounded resigned to it. Luckily we found a beautiful spot situated atop a small rise looking down into the woods just a quarter of a mile further. There was no water, but we had enough to make it through the night. Contentedly, and with a stiff body, Matt settled down for his night in the woods. We laughed about our hike out of town, happy to have our packs off our backs.

I never had any doubt Matt could do what he set out to do. I've watched him grow up, six years older than me, and I've looked up to him all my life. It was a blessing for him to want to be out there with me, sharing an event in my life that I will never forget. We crawled into our tents as thousands of lightning bugs buzzed through the wooded landscape. With 23 miles under his belt, the Googan slept well that night. With the Googan in the tent next to me, I too slept well.

7-8-13

It's about 3am right now. Matt left yesterday morning. On the 6th, we woke up pretty early + knocked out 19. It was a pretty good day—done at about 3. Matt started to freak out a little toward the end of the day, but he did a great job. The views were pretty whack that day. They were all overlooks off the Blue Ridge Parkway. But they were terrible.

Yesterday was a mixed bag. The first 19 miles were fine, but I got drenched my last mile. I tried to frantically set up my tent at a spring as it started raining, but then a downpour began. My tent inside + out was drenched, but I got it set up. It took a bunch of bandana + towel soakings up, but I got it pretty dry. The rain lasted only about an hour, so I could cook at least. But the bugs were horrendous. Hundreds + hundreds of gnats were swarming. I put my bug net on for the first time. While wearing my crocs, something bit my left foot about 10 times too, drawing blood. Not a clue what the hell did that. I got a lot of bites the past couple days and am very itchy right now. Can't wait to get to Buena Vista right now.

It's been kind of raining off + on all night. So I'm afraid to start the day too early + get drenched again. But I can't really sleep. Terrible night.

July 8 Notes: On July 6, Matt's last full day of hiking, we left camp as the sun started to throw its first light over the horizon, licking the edges of the world awake. We wanted to get to camp early and have some time to just hang out and relax. We made camp around 3pm. We enjoyed our surplus of food, rested our feet, and enjoyed each other's company before his departure. Early the next morning, the Googan caught a shuttle back to his car on VA-311. He returned back home with a new respect for hiking and two sore, blistered feet.

Matt took the sun away with him. Toward the end of the day, the skies creaked open and thin drops of rain began to float down. I practically ran the last half mile of trail, determined to reach a water source and make camp before the drizzle turned into a downpour. I reached a spring and frantically raced against the clouds to set up my tent. I was a minute too slow—the skies cracked open as globs of rain poured down on my unprotected tent. By the time I threw on my rainfly and crawled inside, the interior of my shelter was puddled with water. On my hands and knees, I sloshed through the puddles, soaking up the flood with my micro-towel and two bandanas. It took ten minutes before it was dry enough to unfurl my sleeping bag and change into my dry clothes. I huddled myself into my bag and waited for the rain to stop.

As the drops slackened, I climbed out to scan the damage to my gear and clothing. My hiking attire was drenched —I hung it lazily on a line. I knew it wouldn't dry at all. I scanned my surroundings. The spring was rising. I hoped it would not rise into my tent. And as I pulled out my cooking equipment, the gnats came out. They hummed around my head like a pestilent cloud. Some unknown creature drew blood from my foot. I swiped at everything around me and donned my bug net, fighting back frustration as I cooked my meal. A hiker came up the trail. Beads of water still clung to his closely cut brown hair and beard. His shorts, hiking gaiters, and heavy hiking boots were soaked through. He approached me, glancing up at the sky. *Hey, how's it going?* He had a serene look on his face—not a smile, but not a frown either. As my water heated, we talked about nothing in particular. The conversation came to its logical conclusion in the exchange of trail names. *Sir Stooge. You?* He turned away from my pitiful campsite. *Indy. Maybe I'll see you up ahead.*

7-9-13

Punchbowl Shelter: 790.8

Long day—pulled 25 today. Only 11 from Buena Vista, which I'll do tomorrow early morning.

Only got rained on once, for about a minute! Yeah! Finally. There was about a nonstop 3 mile 2k-foot climb toward the end of today. It was really brutal. The climbs today were killer.

So before the one minute of rain, I kept hearing what I thought was thunder. But it was actually some fighter jets training. They must have been pretty far when I thought they were thunder. But then I heard a deafening rumble, and right above me (I was probably 200 ft from the top of the mountain I was on) a jet flew out. The sound was crazy. And it was so close. He was flying really low, so he was super close. Then after he flew, about a mile to the north of me, another flew out, then another minute, and one to the south flew out. It was crazy! That was probably the neatest part of the day.

Anyway, headed to bed since tomorrow morn will be an early one.

July 9 Notes: After days and hours of rain, sixty seconds of it was a beautiful thing. It sheeted down the green hillside, gathering energy like a rolling stone before breaking over me. I pulled on my rain jacket. The drops struck the nylon with dull thuds, hard and dense. Almost immediately, I felt the dirty, thick moisture that seemed to live in my jacket. I pulled it off and tucked it away, glad to feel the cool of the open air. The falling droplets washed away the damp stickiness of the old downpours.

Indy came into camp as the sun's light was disappearing. We anxiously awaited the arrival of a middle aged couple we had passed during our ascent from the James River Footbridge to Punchbowl Shelter. They were in no shape, both physically and mentally, to climb the mountain and arrive at Punchbowl before sunset. We hoped they had turned around and gone back to their car. They never arrived at the shelter.

In the morning, I saw Indy briefly before hitting the trail. He slowly packed up his gear, in no rush to begin the day. Indy preferred to start the day slowly and hike into the setting sun. I, on the other hand, preferred waking early and getting done as soon as I could. I said farewell to him and set out for Buena Vista. Somehow, despite our schedules, we saw each other often, meeting up frequently along the trail and in town. I would make many friends on the trail, but Indy would be one of the best.

7-11-13 *7-12-13

Campsite: 844.0

About 12 or 13 miles from Rockfish Gap. I'll knock those out in the morning nice + early. I'm meeting Uncle Mark + T Man there at noon. So I'm excited for that. I just hope it's not raining tomorrow.

Today was one of those days that feels like it's never ending. I only did about 21 miles, but it felt like more. There was a 6 mile climb, and the gradient was rocky toward the end. So I think those 2 slowed me up + made it feel long.

I've been hiking with Indy the past few days. Cool dude, but a little weird. He's very clingy or something. I don't think he likes being alone. But whatever, he's one of the few thru hikers out here, so it's cool hanging with him.

I think I'm right around Hotshot now too. Not sure what her plan is tomorrow.

Anyway, it's raining again—luckily I'm not wet. Tomorrow should be nice + easy, then some good food with Uncle Mark + Taylor. Sounds good to me! Peace it!

July 12 Notes: Indy's affinity for closeness runs counter to my natural disposition. Although it irked me at first, I came to like it. Despite some of his quirks, which all thru-hikers have, I was drawn to him. Indy was a lot like me—a guy with a solid job who had no real reason to start hiking. And like me, he was looking for something to jar him out of monotony and awaken his spirit. He was a quieter, more contemplative guy than many people on the trail. I think I was drawn to people like that, like Cedric, perhaps because I saw some of myself in them.

The more I got to know Indy, the more I began to feel as though he were a mirror, reflecting back a lot of my own qualities, wishes, and dreams. Unconsciously, I forged an unspoken understanding with what I saw as our shared situation. I was able to look upon him and see my own qualities reflected back at me, untainted by my own mind. I began to see what it was I was doing: I was walking a trail, hoping for something to arise that would change my life forever. I was hoping for something—the wisdom of past ages, or the mental stillness of God—to come shining forth in a burst of light, changing me forever. And I felt that in my search for that tangible *something*, I was damned to fail.

7-13-13 *7-14-13

Loft Mountain Campground: 884.1

Got a few days to catch up on. So, on the 11th, I met the T Man + Uncle Mark at Rockfish Gap. I did about 13 into there. Not a bad hike, pretty standard.

We went to the outfitter quickly to grab me some trail snacks + ask about an issue I had with my poles. So… the night before, some creature ate, yes—ate, the wrist straps of both poles. They were under the vestibule of my tent. Likely mice getting at the salt. So that sucked. The outfitter couldn't help me—I'd have to go to REI.

Anyway, back to T + Uncle Mark. Then we drove a few minutes to Sherando Lake campground. Really nice place. We bbq'd + ate some good food that Aunt B prepared. A flatiron steak, mac + potato salad, + some watermelon. The weather was crap, so when we were done, I was kind of in limbo— what should I do? Uncle Mark proposed me going back home with them for the night. After some thought, I gladly accepted. It'd be nice to get out of the rain. So we went back, ate pizza, got laundry done, etc.

The next day, I went to T's bagel shop for breakfast, updated blog, and surprised Nan + Pop! It was good to see them. Nan made me eat a bunch of food. And luckily Aunt Reen was there. It was good to see her—she looked pretty good. She was tired, but in good spirits. Then Uncle Mark drove me back to the trail in the late afternoon. It was a great visit, and I'm really glad I did it, even though it cost me some miles.

So I started hiking after I got dropped off. My original plan was to night hike and get about 20 miles in. But of course that didn't happen. About 5 miles in, I got drenched. I miserably made it two more miles to a shelter and called it a day. I was not happy. This rain has been crazy. But whatever.

I woke up this morning + hiked 20 to Loft Mountain campground. It's pretty cool here. I walked down to the Wayside and ate a burger + fries. Now I'm sitting at my campsite table, drinking a couple beers, and writing. It's a little weird here. It's kind of between being in town + being on the trail. But it's nice—I just got a shower and am now just hanging.

I'll drink these two beers, brush my teeth, then call it a night. I hear the weather is supposed to be nice this week—fingers crossed!

PS. There are so many deer in this campground. They just walk around like it's no big deal. There's one chilling in the neighboring campground right now.

And now there are two on the other side—about 30 yards away. There's a little fawn too.

Now there's one about 8 yards from me. He sees me, but he's still eating. He's just hanging. Pretty neat.

The one in front of me just circled, coming about five yards from me. He's going toward the fawn + other deer, who are now behind me.

They must be related, the single just interacted with the fawn + the mother. That was all pretty cool. In all, it was probably a 30 or 45 minute affair. That was neat.

The fawn is the only one I see now. He's just staring at me—now he bolted into the woods.

July 14 Notes: I was stuck at Sherando Lake, trying to ignore the spitting skies as I enjoyed my lunch with my uncle and cousin. Somewhat reluctantly, I took the opportunity for a bed, shower, and wash. I knew it would cost me about twenty miles, but with the oppressive threat of more rain, I decided to head to Glen Allen, Virginia. On the way to my aunt and uncle's house, we stopped at the local REI to figure out my trekking pole situation. They let me exchange my old, mouse eaten poles for new ones. It was saddening to hand over my banged up poles. They had been with me for a long time. Scars ran through the metal, scouring the once pristine paint. The cork handles were ragged from falls, and a metal tip had been lost somewhere along the nearly 900 miles I had completed. But I knew my new ones would soon be in the same condition. I was glad to have the black straps around my wrists once more.

Uncle Mark drove me back to Rockfish Gap. I began hiking under clear skies. About a mile in, I took a fall atop a large rock, landing backwards onto my pack. The reality of my break in Glen Allen set in. I had lost a day's worth of hiking—roughly twenty miles. I had once again sacrificed miles for a rest. I set out at a good clip, determined to hike deep into the night to reclaim lost time. But once again, the rain met me. It came first in soft beads, then in blistering sheets. I cursed the futility of washing my clothes at all. I trudged through puddles, soaking my once dry shoes. Mud leapt up to my knees, and my clothes were dirtied and soaked in minutes. I sought no cover, resigned to the fact that I was once again alone, wet, and cold. And that I was entirely helpless to do anything about it. With the rain still falling, and the sun's light leaving Virginia, I decided not to push the hiking into the night. I just wanted to cut my losses, rest my spirit, and sleep.

I set up tent far from the shelter. I wasn't in the mood to talk to anyone. As I peeled off my clothes and got my dinner cooking, I listened for voices but didn't recognize any of my friends. I finished dinner and packed up my food bag. I walked toward the shelter to hang it. There were five hikers there. Sitting at the table was the strange, shaggy haired Caribou and his parents. They were out for a few days with him. An older hiker lay in his sleeping bag in the shelter's loft. He cackled at everything. And a kid of about twenty with a shock of dirty blonde hair was standing near the bear pole. He was short and wiry and he pulled on a cigarette as he listened to the conversation. He seemed like a cold ghost, watching the interactions from another dimension. I introduced myself to Caribou's parents. *Sir Stooge. Nice to meet you.* And with that, the blonde haired wraith-boy came alive, a smile splitting his face.

He introduced himself: *Colonel Patches. I hiked with Tangy before he got off the trail.* He pulled on his cigarette, smoke wreathed his head. I had found the ghostly hiker that I had been tracking since Erwin, Tennessee, and in turn, I had found a friend. Patches grew up on the move—9 states and 15 houses in 16 years. Lasting friends were hard to come by until he moved to Kentucky. He met a kid named Sam and they became brothers. Sam was the healthy one. He never made bad decisions, never drank soda, ran 5 miles every day. And then one morning Sam didn't wake up. They never figured out what killed him. But Sam used to have this imaginary friend growing up named Patches, an evil elf who was always getting into trouble. So when Colonel Patches got on the trail, he became the persona of the elf—the imaginary friend of a dead brother. So the night's misfortunate rain was a blessing in disguise. I had met a new friend, one that I trusted immediately and without reserve. If he was a friend of Tangy's, he was a friend of mine. Unfortunately, Tangy was nowhere to be found on the trail. He was still in Ashville, unsure of his return.

I woke in the morning to heavy skies, but no rain. I pulled on my damp clothes and packed up my gear. In the shelter, I could hear Colonel Patches and the others scuffling about as they woke up. I hiked out alone, knowing he was close behind. I caught Indy the next day, and the three of us headed into the Shenendoahs. I would not write a journal entry for eleven days. Nearly halfway through my trip, the physical and psychological demands were making their mark. What drove Pete, Tangy, and many others from the trail manifested itself differently in me. What for them was physical frustration with the drudgery of the trail, was for me mental frustration with my lack of self understanding: What was I doing out here? What am I missing? In my journal, I wrote down four options for my life after the trail: (1) Teach (2) Get a random job while I search for something else (3) Don't get a shit job (4) Return to Hoboken. I knew that only one was even a real option—the other three were just pen marks to fill up space.

Part II

"It is false to say that humanity is the most excellent being in the universe. The most excellent being in the universe is the universe itself."

—Thomas Berry

7-25-13

Raven Rock Shelter: 1055.0

Ahhh! Haven't written in a long time, I know. It's been tougher + tougher to write. There just aren't enough hours, and there isn't enough energy. Since I started to shoot for 20's every day, the extra time just seems gone. Anyway, let's see what I can recall.

The rest of the Shenendoahs were great. Waysides are amazing! I also had a few decent bear sightings. My first was two cubs, but I couldn't find the mama. That I didn't like. I got a decent picture of one of the cubs.

Then the second was 2 cubs + the mama! About 20 yards or so away. It was really cool. I wasn't scared at all. The mama seemed ok with everything, so I just made noise, made sure she knew me, then kept hiking. No biggie. It was neat though.

What else? Oh—I went into Luray, VA during the SNP (Shenendoah National Park) portion. Cool little town.

I took a zero there. It is a quaint little southern town. Can't complain at all. The only whack thing was when I tried to eat dinner at Uncle Buck's, but the waitress/bartender had too many tables. So in about 50 minutes, saw her once (got a drink) and that was it. I just left after 50 min and went to the Artisan Grille—not a bad place. Otherwise, I had an awesome time there.

However, I didn't enjoy the descent into Thornton Gap (where I went into Luray). It was a long + very rocky descent. I was losing my mind by the bottom. But I survived and got a hitch from this kid + his dad. It looked like they owned a landscaping company. There was a dog in the back who I hung out with the whole way into town. Anyway, they were cool guys.

I'm too tired to write. I'm falling asleep. Will explain tomorrow. Night.

Need to write about: Luray, hitch out; Bear's Den, hiker box; Harper's Ferry; Old South Mt. Inn; Raven's Rock Shelter, coldness; Boiling Springs, Mom and Dad; Boiling Springs w/ Ma + Pa; Lyme Disease!

July 25 Notes: A rumor persisted that once a hiker reached Virginia, he or she wouldn't hit any more mountains. They said it would be as flat as anything I'd ever set my eyes upon, and that I could turn out *at least* twenty miles each day. I am not sure how the "flat Virginia" rumor got started, but I assure you it is not true. It may be flatter than the trail in North Carolina, Tennessee, and Georgia, but *flatter* certainly does not mean *flat.* Towards the end of Virginia, I began to feel the effects of a long distance hike. Physically, I was in excellent shape. My trail legs were strong and my body felt in tune with the daily struggle—my legs drove against the earth and my core sustained my weight. I focused intently on the next landmark, the next water source, the next shelter. But by the time I made camp, I had expended my reserves of daylight, energy, and concentration: the sun deserted me, my body demanded stillness, and my mind worked in a fog of primal needs. I was drained. I knew that sleep would always restore my body's needs. I knew that it would restore even my mental faculties. But sleep didn't always restore my spirit. I had seen it with many hikers. Their will to thru-hike simply subsides. It melts into the trail like yesterday's rain. I didn't know how to guard against that.

Luray was a quiet town. Residents waved happily from front porches or strolled down Main Street. Tourists hopped around town, patronizing the restaurants and shops after seeing the famed Luray Caverns. I spent most of my time with Colonel Patches or alone. I sometimes ran into Caribou and one of his friends who was out for a few days with him. Indy did not go into Luray. He elected to press on to Front Royal, Virginia instead.

On my zero, I felt like I walked almost as much as if I were on the trail. The town was spread out, with everything flanking the few miles of Main Street. The landscaping father and son dropped me off at the southern edge of town, just below main street. I got a room at a hotel on the east edge of town. I walked a couple of miles west to the laundromat, then headed north to the library, then back to my hotel east. The weather was beautiful, my pack was stowed safely in my hotel room, and my legs enjoyed the vigorous activity that they had become accustomed to. Back at the hotel, I took a swim before picking up my first mail drop at the outfitter in town. Throughout my journey, I wasn't very good at getting information to my family and friends about where to send packages. I tended to rely on myself when it came to resupplying in town. The hassle of organizing the contents and location of a mail drop seemed a mental exercise that I often didn't have the energy to undertake. But one thing I missed out on by forgoing mail drops was the morale boosting effect.

Unsure of what to expect from my family, I carried my box back to my hotel room and dumped everything out on the bed. I sorted through personal notes, magazine and newspaper clippings, and lots of food. I read each note slowly and carefully. I read the newspaper clippings, baffled as to the reason for their inclusion in the box, but happy for them all the same. I laughed at a Mutts cartoon that was carefully clipped from the Sunday paper. And lastly, I transferred the golden liquid of a pint of Jack Daniels into a trail-worthy plastic bottle.

7-31

Campsite: 1167.2

So once again, I have slacked on my journal writing. Yes, slacked big time. But let's resume using my notes on the last page.

The hitch out of Luray was really nice + easy. I walked down to the 7-11 on the edge of town, got a donut and a gatorade, then ate it out front. Talked to a couple nice people about the AT, then busted out my sign + stood by the road. Only waited a few minutes before a lady pulled in and asked if I needed a ride. She ran into the 7-11 and left the trunk open for me. I threw my pack in and talked to her son who was in the front seat. He was late teens + had some type of developmental issue. It was fun talking to him. The mother came out and told me another fellow would take me—he was going that way. That nice lady was going to go the wrong way just to drop me off.

The fellow who drove me was a nice guy. He sounded like he had a tough life, but he wasn't bitter. Real nice guy. It's interesting—the types of people who are willing to pick up hikers. They're always legit people. They're never fake or selfish. I like people who pick up hitches.

To be continued—everyone is going to sleep.

July 31 Notes: I saw the woman glance at my sign, thinking about whether or not to pull into the 7-11 parking lot, or to roll on by, as so many other cars do. She looked again and released the gas pedal. She pulled the car gently into the turning lane. *Are you heading out to the AT?* She was short with thick dark hair. *Yea, out to Thornton Gap—to the AT.* She nodded and began to pull into a parking spot. *Let me just grab a coffee first, then I'll bring you back that way.* As I waited for her, I stood outside the car and spoke with her son. He was a neat kid—at some points difficult to understand. But I was happy for him, considering the woman who was his mother. She came back outside, coffee in hand. *There's a fella in there who said he'll take you back that way. He's headed that way anyway.* I realized that she was going to drive me out there for no other reason than to help me out. *I need to head into town.* I thanked her for her willingness to help and said goodbye to the boy. I pulled my pack from the trunk. A man stood next to a pickup truck a few parking spaces away. He waved me over. I tossed my pack into the truck bed and jumped into the messy front seat. He was a middle aged man with flecks of silver beginning to show on his head and mustache. He drove sternly with both hands high on the wheel. The truck hugged the flowing curves of the road and he kept both eyes locked forward. He never turned to look at me as he told me his story, unwilling to share the burden of his pain through his eyes. In the past year, his well caved in, his brother tragically passed away, and he had very little money to speak of. But with his past upon him, he still treated his future as a blessing, happy to be alive and happy to help a hiker out.

As we reached my destination, I pulled some money from my wallet. He refused it, pushing it back toward me. Instead, he just shook my hand and said, *Be good to your family.* I climbed from the truck, grabbed my pack, and waved goodbye. It is bittersweet to greet a person as a stranger, and in fifteen minutes, say farewell as a friend. I really appreciate people like that man. I know all hikers do.

8-1-13

501 Shelter: 1189.3

So anyway, the hitch out of Luray was good.

Luray was a neat town too. I'm glad I zeroed there. I sealed my tent, swam in the pool, went to a nice breakfast joint. The only bad thing was the dinner I had my zero day. I went to Uncle Jo's (or something like that). I waited at the bar for about an hour, only seeing the bartender once to order a beer. I never had a chance to order food, so I up + left. But other than that, Luray was great. I hung with Colonel Patches and Caribou mostly.

So then I was back to the trail. We hit a couple of really hot days (but at least the rain stopped), and I crushed the Roller Coaster. It wasn't nearly as bad as I thought it would be. In the middle of the Roller Coaster, I stayed at the Bear's Den hostel. That was a cool place. Well kept by the PATC (Potomac Appalachian Trail Club)—had nice bunks, pizza, and ice cream. Can't beat that. I met Father there. Super interesting dude—he's a priest from Poland. Colonel Patches made a hilarious food concoction for dinner that I snacked on. It was actually not too bad—hot dogs, chili, veg, and some other stuff. In the morning, a family who was staying in a cabin on the grounds cooked us breakfast. Got a late jump—but it was well worth it.

I also got some awesome stuff out of the hiker box at Bear's Den. I got a couple of Mountain Houses and some Clif Bars. It was awesome but weird. Because I checked the hiker box when we first got there, and there was nothing good. Then boom, next morning all this awesome stuff was in there. Colonel Patches got some good stuff too.

So from the hostel, after the awesome breakfast, I headed into Harper's Ferry—the unofficial halfway point!

It was a good time in Harper's Ferry. I stayed at the Teahorse Hostel two nights. The night I first got there I didn't do too much. Just walked around a dead town (Sunday night) then got some food + beers from 7-11. I was hanging with Colonel Patches + Indy. Colonel Patches left the next day to head home. He's doing 2 big sections, finishing up next summer. Which sucks—I liked hanging with Colonel Patches.

Anyway, on my zero I ran my errands, went to Pvt. Quinn's Pub for lunch and got some sweet shirts for the whole family. I shipped them home along with my sleeping bag. What else did I do? I checked out some free mini museums. They were neat. Harper's Ferry has some really neat history behind it. I could definitely go back there for a couple days at some point. After spending some time in town, I went to the library all the way on the other side of town. Then I went back into town to eat dinner before everything closed. It's crazy—everything in that town closes by 8pm, and most places close at like 5pm. But anyway, I went to a nice bar and had some beers + dinner, all in about 35 minutes. Overall, neat place.

Super funny story about the owner of the Teahorse. She was a very nice, but very strange woman. She was great though. So the second night there, we got caught casually drinking a couple of beers—against hostel rules. She disallows alcohol because she doesn't want to be the "party hostel." Let alone that she is the only hostel in town. So she catches us, and kind of scolds us, and slams the door on the way out. I felt like I was in grade school again. It was funny, but we felt bad as well —we knew the rules.

So the next morning she was back to her nice self, and she pulled me aside to tell me what a nice personality I have, and that I should tell my mother so. I said I would, I'll call her soon. Then she went into a short monologue that made me feel bad. She said her kids don't often call her, but she understands because they have their own lives. I told her they should still call. It was a nice conversation. I don't think she opens up much, so it was nice to get that compliment and be a part of that conversation. Great lady—strange, but I liked her.

And one more thing about the Teahorse. She makes waffles every morning for the tenants. They're delicious. Anyway, the first morning, she had to shuttle someone somewhere, so I took over as waffle maker at her request. It was an honor to iron that waffle batter.

So, left Harper's Ferry + broke into Maryland. Crazy. Maryland was pretty uneventful. Bud attempted the 4 state challenge—failed. Hotshot succeeded, then did 5 more—she pulled a 50 in about 20+ hours. She is completely insane.

Me, Indy, + Uno ate dinner at the South Mountain Inn one night. That was fun—had a few beers + some good food. It was a classy joint, but luckily empty. We sat at the bar and hung with the bartender, she was cool.

But like I said, I was in + out of Maryland quickly. Pennsylvania had some big time events though. First was a series of bad nights. I sent my +15 sleeping bag home in Harper's Ferry, and lo + behold, I received 3 amazingly cold nights at the start of PA. Someone said one night got down into the 40's. Needless to say, I couldn't sleep. I would be warm enough until about 1am, then just not be able to sleep. So I just started hiking. It was around 4am when I started those few days. It was brutal. But it was nice to get miles in nice + early. But damn, it was cold.

Then Mom + Dad met me in Boiling Springs! It was a blast seeing them. First, the good stuff from that weekend. Mom brought me tons of awesome food, we drank and ate + hung. Patches (the girl) and Indy were hanging with us. It was a great day. Then Sunday Mom + Dad hiked 8 miles with me to Carlisle. Then us three + Indy went to a bar and had lunch and I watched some US soccer game. Mom + Dad got some sweet trail magic from some folks at the bar who took them back to Boiling Springs to the car. Me + Indy on the other hand took an hour to hitch back to the trail.

And I felt like crapola Sunday night. So here is the bad news. Saturday while talking to Matt on the phone (he + Dana are having a baby!!! Woohoo!!!) I noticed a rash on my right calf. It somewhat looked like a bullseye. So after some research + consulting with Ma + Pa + Patches (her mom is a nurse), I decided to go to the ER early Sunday morning. Thank God Mom + Dad were there so they could drive me from Boiling Springs to Carlisle's ER. So I felt fine all day Sunday. I got antibiotics, a tetanus shot, and they took blood for a test. Everything was great—got the prescription quickly. And boom, out on the trail at 10am. So then, right after Mom + Dad left, around 4pm, I started to feel like crap. Tired, achy, + restless—flu-like. Me + Indy hiked about 2 miles out of Carlisle before I couldn't do it anymore. I had a terrible sleep, tossing + turning all night. I was so achy I could barely move. So I woke up Monday + still felt pretty blah, but well enough to hike. By the time I made it to Duncannon at about 5pm, I felt fine. I think the antibiotics hadn't kicked in yet and I started to get some symptoms Sunday night. The rash also started to heal, but it made it look worse. It kind of bruised as it healed, so it became darker + more distinct. Which looked bad, but was probably good. I feel fine now, so the antibiotics must be winning. It just sucks now because I can't drink much. Just a drink or two. But oh well—at least I'm not sick.

So now Paul is meeting me tomorrow—and Steve Olson. I'm going to take a break. Will write more soonish.

August 1 Notes: During the Roller Coaster, a thirteen mile stretch of closely packed ascents and descents, the rain of the past month and a half gave way to a scorching heat wave. Soaked in my own sweat after traversing the sharp rises and falls, I walked through the gates of Bear's Den hostel. Bear's Den stands just above Snickers Gap. It is a castle like structure built by a wealthy professor back in the 1930s. I unloaded my gear in the bunk room downstairs. After a shower, I went upstairs to the kitchen to consume a delicious frozen pizza. After eating the entire circle of sausage, pepperoni, olives, and peppers, Colonel Patches forced me to consume some of the stewy concoction he created. To my surprise, it wasn't bad at all, but my busting gut couldn't take any more food. I rested my tired body for an hour or two before opening up a pint of ice cream. Colonel Patches, Father, and I lazed around, getting to know the building and the caretakers there. The caretakers struggled through laughter as they told us about the wedding the day before. The bride, wearing a tiara, and groom, wearing jean shorts, were happily married on the mountainside as the tunes of Led Zeppelin carried over the gap. I wish I was there for that.

The next morning, Father left as the sun rose. Colonel Patches and I hung around for several hours to eat the breakfast that the family had made for us. There were three generations of the family present—about eight people in all. They were kind, giving people. They prepared the meal for us for the simple reason that they wanted to. I appreciated their hospitality, and I know Colonel Patches did as well. After my goodbyes, I packed up and hit the trail, intent on reaching Harper's Ferry at a decent hour. The twenty miles to Harper's Ferry dragged by slowly. Drained, and ready for my zero, I took a break on the hill above the Shenendoah River, about two miles from town. I rested on a log and drank my final swigs of the whiskey my brother had sent to me in Luray. It was a celebration of what I had accomplished so far, and a prayer to what I would accomplish in the future. I tipped the plastic bottle high, drained the last sip along with some flecks of dried leaves, picked up my pack, and made my way down. I wasn't sure what it would be like entering town. I was hoping for a big brass band and some locals to cheer me on as I walked out of the woods and into society. I got nothing of the sort. I didn't see any white blazes anywhere. Like a whirling dervish, I backtracked and spun around a few times before realizing I had to climb a short set of stairs to the campus of Storer College. I gained my bearings, and made my way toward Washington Street. I broke down my trekking poles, clipped them to my chest, and pulled out my tennis ball. After almost three months of hiking, I had the privilege of walking the streets of Harper's Ferry—the midway point of the Appalachian Trail. I opened the door to the Teahorse Hostel. No matter what happened from here on out, I had at least made it here.

Sir Stooge, I said. Laurel, the owner of the Teahorse Hostel, burst out laughing. *And your real name? Chris Quinn?* she said in her quietly kind voice. *That's funny, there's another Chris here.* She looked at her paperwork. *His trail name is Indy. Do you know him?* For the past several days, Indy had been fifteen or so miles ahead of me. Two days prior, he succumbed to the dry heat and the Roller Coaster. Dizzy and confused, he spent a day at the Blackburn Trail Center, recovering from dehydration. During that time, I made up the miles he had on me, catching him in Harper's Ferry. *Well, he just got in here earlier today. I think he went into town a bit ago. You may see him there.* I thanked her and headed upstairs to wash up.

After settling into the hostel, I walked into town to check things out and search for Indy. Being a Sunday night, there was not much activity in Lower Town, the main area of Harper's Ferry. As I looked for any open bar or restaurant to grab a bite to eat, I spotted Indy down the hill. Since nothing was left open, we started back toward the hostel. As we neared our destination, we found Colonel Patches eating a whole pizza on the steps of a pizza shop. He had gotten there just as it was closing, and after some pleading, they conjured up a pizza for him. As Colonel Patches ate, we walked over to 7-11, got a few beers and some food, and headed back to the hostel.

The Teahorse is an interesting mix between B&B and hostel. It is clean, quaint, and welcoming. But it still retains the communal feel of a hostel. After staying at a lot of more spartan hostels along the trail, the Teahorse was a nice departure into the realm of the cozy. We drank our beers, hiding them in coffee mugs for fear of being caught by Laurel. But as she made her late night run through the kitchen, preparing everything for the next morning's waffle breakfast, she spotted a group of other hikers openly drinking beers. In words of restrained anger, she berated us for breaking hostel rules before slamming the door on the way out. We finished our beers and went to bed.

By the morning, Laurel was back to her old self. She seemed to have forgiven us for the night before. We had breakfast happily, scarfing down a massive amount of waffles. On my zero, I did my errands and found some time to just hang out and grab some good food and drink. Indy and I went to a little pub called Private Quinn's for lunch. I was hoping for some special discount due to the fact that I shared the same surname as the pub. Instead, they just told me that a lot of Quinns came through there—so I settled for paying the tab in its entirety. I visited the library, writing a draft of a blog post called *Alone*. Indy, Bud, Colonel Patches, and I spent our last night in Harper's Ferry just hanging around, doing nothing in particular.

Bud was close with Boo Bear and Wash, the two brothers from down south. The three of them hiked and aqua blazed together through all of Virginia. Through the two misfit brothers, I got to know Bud a little bit while we were in Tennessee and Virginia. He's a respectable Nashville gentleman in his mid twenties—deep voiced, intelligent, and quietly spiritual. He was big and strong, with a scruffy beard and short brown hair. I would see Bud periodically throughout the trail and although I never got to know him as well as some others, I always enjoyed his company and his benevolent demeanor. Bud was up for anything, as evidenced by his unreal attempt at the Four State Challenge. The Four State Challenge is an undertaking that few hikers are willing to put themselves through. In a 24 hour period, a hiker will attempt to hike about 45 miles from the VA/WV border a bit south of Harper's Ferry to the MD/PA border, setting foot in four states during a single day. The next morning, as Bud hiked south out of Harper's Ferry to reach West Virginia and the start of the Four State Challenge, Indy, Uno, and I hiked north toward Dahlgren Backpack Campground, situated next to the Civil War battlefield of the Battle of South Mountain. We wished Bud luck, waved farewell to Harper's Ferry, and set off into Maryland.

The first time I met Uno, somewhere in northern Virginia, his shoes were in shambles. He had cut away the entire heel of his right shoe because of blistering. His hair was shorn close to his head, and he wore a large, scruffy beard. On his lean body was a cut off shirt. All of his clothing was highlighted with bright, fluorescent colors. On his head, he wore an old running hat, darkened by sweat and dirt. His attire and aura of rebellion made me somewhat suspicious of him, although that feeling quickly faded. He was odd—in the quirky, adolescent way of a grungy rebel. Our hike to Dahlgren was easy. We took our time, walking easily and reading the monuments that border the battlefield of the Battle of South Mountain. We made camp around 6pm, then made the short walk to the South Mountain Inn, a restaurant and bar situated a half mile off the trail. After trying to make ourselves look more presentable, we walked into the Inn, hoping they wouldn't kick us out for our slovenly appearance. Without a mention of our attire, the bartender happily served us. We spent a couple of hours there, snacking on burgers and some lox, (first time Indy or Uno ever had lox!). After dinner, we made our way back to the campground. As we crawled into bed, we spotted a tent that had popped up while we were at the Inn. It was Bud. After covering only twenty miles of the Four State Challenge, he called off his ill-fated attempt and settled in for some much needed rest of the ego. Rightfully so, we had some jokes at his expense the next morning.

I made my way through Maryland and into Pennsylvania. In Boiling Springs, Pennsylvania, I met up with my mother and father. The first night there, Mom and Dad took me, Indy, Patches, and a friend of Boo Bear and Wash's named Hummingbird out to dinner. The next morning, my parents and I had breakfast with Fiddlehead, who I had seen on and off throughout the trail. Although I wish they could have met them all—Munchies, Tangy, Hotshot, Bud, Colonel Patches, Jupiter, and even Music Man (who I had last seen limping around somewhere in Virginia where he told me in his cartoonish ramble that he had been stepped on by a horse), I know they relished the opportunity to meet even just a few—to hear their stories, and to get to know the kinds of people I had been living with.

But along with the good times came a scary moment. The tick bite scare was a roadblock that I conquered as fluidly as I could. It was not fun, but I, with the help of my friends and family, came away perfectly healthy. A couple of weeks later, I got the results of my blood work back. It turned out that I didn't have any Lyme antibodies at all. I am unsure what it was that made me feel so sick as I left Carlisle. As I recovered from the tick bite, news of my health scare spread amongst the trail community. I showed the darkening bullseye to any hikers who wished to see it. The mark became a kind of prophetic symbol: a warning and a sign of what it means to be a thru-hiker.

I made my way through Pennsylvania, catching up with Patches and Hotshot again. For the first time in a long time, I felt close to home, both physically and emotionally. I soon found myself sitting at a road crossing near Port Clinton, awaiting the arrival of my brother Paul, and my buddy Steve, aka Scuba Springsteen.

And one more thing about the monuments that stand at the battlefield of the Battle of South Mountain. As Indy, Uno, and I walked about the cluster of memorials that stood at the fringe of the killing field, I saw a quote on the memorial of the mortally wounded Union General Jesse L. Reno. As he lay dying, he saw his good buddy, and he cried out to him, "Hallo, Sam, I'm dead!" Sam thought it a dark and unnecessary joke. But Reno clarified, whispering to his dear friend, "Yes, yes. I am dead—good bye!" He died several minutes later. I laughed with Reno and cried with Sam. I hope, in the end, I have courage enough to battle for each breath—clinging proudly to the silent hum of life that fades from my body—because there is something miraculous in the very act of living. But when it is all said and done—when it is all over and there is only the faintest remnant of life left in my flesh—I hope I also have courage enough to embrace death as wholly as she embraces me: with the bitterness of the fight removed, and the knowledge that Nothingness will remain.

But hopefully, that time is still a long ways off.

8-2-13

Game Commission Road: 1199.1

So, I am currently at a road crossing awaiting Paul + Steve's arrival. But I'll get to that in a bit.

Where I left off was my sick Sunday night. It was

terrible. But luckily, midday on Monday I felt pretty good. I made it into Duncannon without too much trouble, arriving about 4pm. Hotshot, Indy, + Juno all stayed at the Doyle. Uno + Lotus did too actually

The Doyle was hilarious. Downstairs was a bar + food —decent. And upstairs was a super seedy, crappy motel. It had a lot of character, I must say. But it's one of those places you need to visit. It was a fun experience.

We all just hung that night, drank a few beers, then crashed. Breakfast was great. We ate across the street at this diner kind of joint. I got some huge and delicious blueberry pancakes.

The next day was a long one, around 25 or so. Then the day after that we finished at 501 Shelter. Super cool shelter. Fully enclosed with a solar shower. You can order food to get delivered. I got a small calzone, small hoagie, + some bacon ranch fries. It was an awesome night.

Me, Hotshot, Patches, + Indy all stayed the night there. We woke up to some nasty rain, and group think took over, and next thing we knew we were taking a zero on a shuttle to Port Clinton. The weather was hikeable, but nasty. So a zero wasn't necessary, but whatever.

I got some new shoes at Cabela's—the Bare Access 2's. There's a lot more thickness on the sole, which is helping out big time on these rocks. Not as minimalist as the TG 1's, but nice shoes. I've definitely liked them so far. They're more like cross training shoes than trail runners.

The zero was decent though. Good food, drink, + sleep.

Today is the day after the zero, and I've done about 9 miles. Now I await the arrival of those two stooges. We only have about 15 into Port Clinton, so I don't want to do too many tonight. Maybe just a couple. Then we'll cruise into Port Clinton tomorrow.

I'm finally caught up! Going to eat something and call home, then Paul should almost be here.

August 2 Notes: I stepped out of the green tunnel and onto a vacant, paved road. I clipped my trekking poles to my pack, pulled out my tennis ball, and bounced my way into

Duncannon, past old car dealerships, decrepit homes, and failing infrastructure. I walked up to the Doyle Hotel—a haunted looking structure on a corner spot in town. As I neared the doors, a large, boisterous woman walked out, wiping her hands on a bar towel. *Come on in! Someone is in here waiting for you.* She turned back inside. I swung open the doors. My eyes adjusted to the dingy darkness of the place and I saw Hotshot waving at me from a table. I hadn't seen her in several weeks. I dropped my pack and took a seat at the table beside her. After catching up over some greasy food and a beer, she told me she was planning on hiking out that day. I broke her down with the help of Indy, who came in soon after me, and Juno, a small, placid woman I had met a couple of days prior. She decided to spend the night at the Doyle. After showers and some rest, we grabbed dinner at the Doyle before moving to another bar down the street. We saddled up to the bar: me, Indy, Hotshot, Uno, and Lotus, a small girl with short, spunky hair. To my left sat some drunk old local. He talked my ear off about his hiking days, Trail Angel Mary, and the weather. He bought us all beers.

The next morning, all of us hiked out. I was happy to leave Duncannon behind. A sense of overbearing depression hangs heavily over that town. I loved it for what it was, but I just couldn't stay too long. The trail now took me through rocky trails swarming with Timber Rattlesnakes and Copperheads. At one point, I was held up by a rattlesnake that blocked my path for ten minutes, defying my attempts to get it to move. The snakes throughout Pennsylvania kept me on my toes. But for Indy, who took his name from the famous Harrison Ford character who despises snakes, they scared the hell out of him during several encounters.

The following night, Hotshot, Indy, and I caught up with Patches, and we all settled in for the night at 501 Shelter. Like Partnership Shelter, it's one of the few shelters you can order food for delivery. Needless to say, we took full advantage of the opportunity. A fire was made, and we settled into the large, enclosed structure. Following 501 Shelter, the foursome of Patches, Hotshot, Indy, and myself hung out around the Port Clinton/Hamburg area on our zero. We got a couple of rooms at the Port Clinton Hotel and spent hours at Cabela's. I picked up some new shoes. Patches bought a camouflage bikini. Then we resupplied and stocked up on some wine to spend our zero with. We spent the zero lazily, drinking our wine and watching the television. Hotshot came down with an illness of some kind. I think her body just needed time to recover from the Four State Challenge. She never really took a break after completing the challenge, choosing to push through the next days without a zero until Port Clinton. She spent the evening and all night in bed with Patches as her guardian. The next day, she was back in action. We took a shuttle back to 501 Shelter and continued our journey.

I sat on a rock at PA-183, writing in my journal. I looked up as a car roared around the bend in front of me—cars move so fast. Then I looked down at my new shoes, the only method of transportation I had. I prodded the mesh material that covered the upper part of the foot. Then I ran my dirtied fingers under the thickness of the cushioned soles. They had just started to break in, and luckily the transition had not caused much discomfort at all. I turned back to my journal and began to write. Just as the ink began to fall from the point, Hotshot prodded me out of my paper dreams. I looked up at her. *Where you going tonight?* She put on her sunglasses now that she was out of the shade. *I'd like to get to Port Clinton. But maybe I'll just go up to that next shelter, like six or seven away. What are you doing?* She wasn't going to stick around, but I decided to ask anyway. *My brother and my buddy are coming. I'm meeting them here. You can hang out and camp with us tonight. We're probably only going about two or three more from here—I don't want to push too far. We're going to spend tomorrow in town.* She nodded back at me. *They should be here within twenty minutes or so. Then we're just going to hang out all night. Hang with us.* She hesitated, flipped the idea around in her head. *Eh. Maybe. I kind of want to get to Port Clinton tonight though.* I smirked, I already knew that would be her answer. *Come on. Just hang.* She turned on her heel and looked north across the road. *You'll just have to catch me again!* Hotshot missed out that night, but she probably wouldn't have been able to hang with the amount of stooginess that occurred anyway— we crushed a bunch of food, got lost looking for the Black

Swatara Spring, and failed at making a sustained fire. On that beautiful night, as the smoke of the failing fire rose into the night sky, Stooge City Central, population 3, was located fourteen miles outside of Port Clinton, Pennsylvania.

8-7-13

Rattlesnake Spring: 1302.8

Tonight is the first night in a while that I've had some time to relax + write. Weird.

So I'm a little bit outside of Delaware Water Gap, PA. Which means—I'm in New Jersey!

It's been a little crazy since Paul's trip, but here's the rundown:

So I met Paul + Steve at that road. Then we just hiked a couple miles to a nice little campsite. We got set up + chilled the rest of the night. We ate lots of food (thanks Grandma) and tried to make a fire. It didn't do too well—wood was too wet. Fun night though.

Saturday was our main hiking day. We did about 14 or so into Port Clinton. It was a decent hike. We got rained on most of the time, but luckily it was pretty light. The rocks were alright. Nothing overly terrible. Paul + Steve had a good time. I think Paul really enjoyed it. We threw a bunch of rocks off a view point toward the end of the hike! That was fun.

Once we got back to the car, we attempted to get a real hotel room in Hamburg, but failed. They were all booked up for whatever reason. So... back to the Port Clinton Hotel it was. That place is hilarious. We got showered up and had a few drinks there, then headed to Pappy T's in Hamburg. It was a cool place, but it was dead. I don't think the Port Clinton/Hamburg area is a jumping night life place. We played some Buck Hunter + pool, drank, and had some food. It was a fun night, even if it wasn't a raging Saturday night.

Sunday, Paul + Steve hiked about 6 miles out of Port Clinton with me. Then we parted, as they headed back to the car in town.

I think Paul had a lot of fun. I'm glad he did. And Steve loved being out there again. He had a blast.

I am falling asleep and it's 7pm. I am exhausted—I'll need to write the rest later. Night.

August 7 Notes: Grandma sent a huge supply of food with Paul and Scuba Springsteen. On top of the trail staples I had come to love—peanut butter, tortillas, energy bars, Ramen, and the rest—Grandma gave us some fresh fruit! If there is one thing I craved while on the trail, it was raw fruits and vegetables. After days of consuming processed, packaged, and dehydrated meals, the raw coolness of a watery veggie or juicy fruit was an amazing experience. After snacking on some of the food, we got lost trying to find the spring, eventually found it, then set up our tents. We set up our cooking sets and dug into our meals and snacks, intent on eating as much as we could to keep the weight off our backs. As we finished our dinners, our fire, saturated with the rainfall of previous days, sent up steaming wisps of smoke. Steve shared stories of his thru-hike the previous year. He is a laid back kid in his early twenties. With short dark hair, he is well built, but he is so kindly you don't notice his stature at first. His wide, cheery eyes casually take in everything around him, whether man or nature. But his heart takes in everything as though it were all new. Each time I see him it's as if I haven't seen him for years. As he chomped on his third or fourth peanut butter bar, he told us about his plans to hike out west in the coming months. The night, like our dead fire, soon slipped away. We crawled into our tents, excited for sleep and tomorrow's hike. Paul, in his struggles to acclimate to the trail, had a rough night. He heard whispers of witches calling through the trees to him—*We're going to get you Paul!* And at one point, he woke up in a panic. His tent was coming down around him. He thrashed and fought the binding nylon. But he soon discovered it was not his failing tent. It was only his sleeping bag snugged up against his body. Relieved, he sunk back into sleep, the witches whispering.

The next day, we hiked through spitting rain. We took our time, enjoying the chance to be kids again, throwing rocks from a view point. We hiked into Port Clinton, drove around Hamburg looking for a hotel, failed, and got a room at the Port Clinton Hotel, where Indy, Hotshot, Patches, and I had spent the night a few days earlier. We threw down our packs and showered. We headed to a bar in Hamburg. It wasn't exactly what we were looking for. The bar was decent—a standard sports bar with pool tables, a few arcade games, and decent food. But there were only about eight other people in the whole place. The next morning, Paul and Steve hiked about five miles north with me. At a spring, we stalled for time, not wanting to separate. We said our goodbyes and they turned back south, toward the car, and toward home. I watched them for as long as possible. I swung my pack onto my back, and hiked on. The next few miles were tough. I no longer had Paul and Steve, and I was at least a day behind Indy, Patches, and Hotshot. The past few days had been great, but now I crashed into a depression—I felt desperately alone. I missed my friends, I missed my family, and I missed my home.

Note: From the next entry until August 28, my journal dates are off by one whole month. The real month is August, but the journal entries are labeled as July. The dates become correct again when I reach my last entry in August.

7-8-13 *8-8-13

Mashipacong Shelter: 1326.5

One more thing I forgot about Paul's visit. His trail name is "Solitaire." He borrowed a hilarious Eureka! tent from his buddy. And it was called a Solitaire. So he became Solitaire.

So after Steve + Paul left, I was a little bit behind Hotshot, Indy, + Patches. So I got pretty explosive in order to catch up to them at Delaware Water Gap, PA. One of those days I pulled my longest day—34 miles! It was pretty brutal. And it was over a lot of crappy Pennsylvania rocks. I started at about 6am and finished about 11pm. The terrain didn't help my time. Nor did the guy sleeping in his hammock at mile 32 who scared the hell out of me.

This may be the most scared I've been in a very long time. I was just cruising along with my head lamp, looking at my footing. Mind you, night hiking is weird—you feel drugged for some reason. So I'm cruising along, head down, and really close to me, I hear a man half gasping, half yelling in a panicked, fearful tone. My blood ran cold. I got the chills and my voice left me. I looked up to see a guy about 8 ft from me flailing around in his hammock, continuing to yell for about 5 seconds. I remember repeatedly saying, "It's ok" although it felt like it wasn't coming from me. Eventually he woke up I guess, and apologized. He said he was having a bad dream, and he heard things around him, and I scared him obviously. So all ended well. He was nice. He hilariously said, "Well, maybe I'll see you tomorrow." Didn't see him.

It was terrifying though. I haven't been that scared in a while. What made it worse was that it was so similar to a recurring nightmare I used to have. In the nightmare, I'd be crawling, not walking, through the woods at dusk, not night, and I'd eventually see something in front of me. And looking up, I'd see a creature/monster of some kind that would make a yell/scream. It's eerie how similar it was. That terrified me though. I can understand how people go into shock from fear. I think I was in it for 5 seconds.

So anyway, I finished my 34 and caught Indy + his wife. Then the next day I caught Patches + Hotshot in town. We all went to dinner at the diner. Data was there too. It was a fun night. Patches started some liberal rants which were funny. I kept my mouth shut.

The next morning, most people headed out early. I went to the diner for breakfast—can't pass up a meal. So I'm behind Patches + Hotshot now. Indy zeroed in Water Gap. His wife's parents were picking her up on the zero.

So that's that. It's storming out now. Hopefully it will pass by the morning though. We shall see.

August 8 Notes: The light of my headlamp swayed softly. It illuminated rocks and branches for just a moment, just long enough for me to decide on my next few steps, then a new swath of trail would come into the light as the old faded back to darkness. I was in a foggy headed trance. The light swayed, my breath was even and quiet, the trail seemed to never change —just rocks and roots, roots and rocks. I was 32 miles into my longest day. Only two more to go. I was hungry, thirsty, and tired.

It was a hollow, breathy scream—as if all the air in his lungs was forced from his mouth out of pure fear. It went quiet for a split second as he breathed in more air, then forced it out as rapidly as it came in—hollow and breathy. I whirled my light toward the sound, and to my horror, I saw a man, wide eyed and fearful, as he thrashed about in his hammock. Words came out of my mouth, although they seemed to make no noise. My eyes swam in my head—I had trouble focusing on the terror that flailed in the hammock. The screams pushed their way out of the man, and the silent words left me. After several seconds, the wide eyes shrunk, and the hollow yells turned to ragged breathing. My hands were out in front of me, in defense or of pleading I wasn't sure. *It's ok.* I finally heard my words.

Oh man. He returned to waking consciousness. *Oh man. I'm sorry man. I was having a bad dream, and I thought I heard something back over there, then I must have heard you. Oh man, I'm sorry man.*

I felt my hands drop to my sides, my weight on my poles. My swimming eyes focused on the man in his hammock. I tried to get the floating feeling out of my limbs. *Jese, it's ok dude. You scared the hell out of me though. My God man. You scared the hell out of me.*

Sorry dude. Oh man, I'm sorry. You ok? Ok, well sorry man. I'm on these meds for pain in my knee and all. Sorry man. I stood there awkwardly for a moment before my feet began to move.

It's fine dude. I'm good.

Ok. Well, maybe I'll see you tomorrow?

Ok, see you tomorrow. I set off down the trail, the swaying light illuminating the rocks and roots upon which I had no choice but to walk, horrified, through the never-ending, unchanging darkness of the trail. I sucked at my water bladder, trying to pull the remnants of water that clung to the inner walls. After two more miserable miles, I made it to Leroy A. Smith Shelter. I got water, immediately drank two liters, and then set up my tent by headlamp, careful not to disturb the only other tent that sat forty feet from me across the clearing. I settled into my bag, glad to be afraid and not dead.

Thirty four miles over rocky Pennsylvania wasn't the brightest idea I had on the trail. The primary reason I pulled a 34 mile day was to get caught up to Indy, Patches, and Hotshot. The tent that I shared the clearing with that night was actually Indy and his wife, Haley. She was out visiting him for a few days on the trail. The three of us made the push into Delaware Water Gap the next day, arriving in the late afternoon. The other reason I hiked 34 miles was to find the trail's most precious resource—water. Originally, I was going to do about 30 to the Stempa Spring, get water, and make camp anywhere I could. It was dark by the time I reached the spring, so with my headlamp, I walked 0.6 miles down a steep side trail to the spring. Upon reaching it, I discovered it was dry. With little energy left to burn on self-pity, I immediately turned around and hiked the 0.6 miles back to the AT, then two miles to where I got scared by the hammock man, then two miles to the shelter. It was a disheartening and terrifying hike through the night. In all, I probably did about 37 miles that day, although only 34 of them were Appalachian Trail miles. But water and friends are always worth the hike.

I spent a day in Delaware Water Gap, then hiked out behind Patches and Hotshot, headed for Unionville, Pennsylvania.

7-10-13 *8-10-13

Cascade Brook: 1364.7

So that storm lasted the whole night. I pitched my tent in a bad spot. I got a nice puddle near the left side of my tent. Got some leakage. So the entire inside of my tent was pretty saturated. But it didn't matter much because it poured all morning, so everything was wet anyway. But I trucked through it.

A lot of the trails were flooded and some streams were absolutely raging. There were a couple crossings that made me a little nervous—but I survived. It was a wet morning, but it was actually kind of fun.

When I reached Unionville, I went to the General Store, then to the bar. I had dinner and some beers at the bar. And as a nice bonus, I sat out a passing storm. So I was there for a while—about 3 hours.

Then I hiked out about 5 miles to the shelter. Overall, it was a decent day despite the pouring rain in the morning.

Today I did about 18 or something like that. I'm a couple miles from the lot where I'll meet Mom + Dad in the morning. So tomorrow should be good.

I also ran into Eli + his wife (I forget her name—their trail names are Cannon + Lady). I hadn't seen them since about a week into the trip—crazy. They're cool though. I hiked the second half of the day with them.

I also had lunch at a sweet little farm market. It reminded me a bit of Johnson's. I got an Italian hoagie—and it was enormous + delicious. Anyway, time for bed. Tomorrow will be a fun day. Later!

August 10 Notes: I spent a bit more time at Wit's End, the bar in Unionville, than I had originally planned. The beers and food got me inside and the passing rainstorm kept me there. I sat down at the end of the bar, careful not to disturb the social balance of the locals. They sent periodic glances my way, cognizant of the fact that I was an outsider. They were not glances of suspicion or intimidation however—merely of the knowledge that I was not one of them. I charged my phone and drank and ate in relative silence, only speaking when ordering from the bartender, a young girl with dark hair. After my second beer, one of the locals spun in his chair and asked me if I was hiking the trail. *Yes I am.* A short conversation began and ended. I finished my meal, paid my bill, and thanked the bartender before stepping outside. Just as I did, a wall of rain rushed down the street, threatening my pack, which I had left under an awning out front. I quickly ran down to my pack, jammed it as far under cover as possible, then ran back inside. *I'm back. No way I'm going out in that. I've dealt with too much rain already.* She poured me a shot of Jameson. *You better have one of these then.* I stayed at Wit's End for another half hour as the storm passed. This time for good, I waved farewell to Wit's End and headed back to the trail.

The rain, beers, and burgers had hindered my progress a little bit. I struggled to catch up to my friends, lagging just a day or two behind them. I pushed hard into Greenwood Lake, New York, hoping to catch them before meeting up with my mom, dad, sister, and my buddy Neil, who would hike with me for several days. Instead of finding Indy, Hotshot, and Patches, however, I found Cannon and Lady. Soon after our reunion, Cannon, Lady, and I sat on a rock overlooking Greenwood Lake. An American flag, carried up by some unknown hiker, flew stiffly in the breeze. I snapped a couple of pictures of the young couple with Cannon's camera. We passed around a cocktail of Dr. Pepper and vodka. We talked about how we first met: the second night on the trail, way back in Georgia at Gooch Gap Shelter. The conversation brought to mind the early days on the trail and my time spent with Munchies and Tangy.

It struck me then: I had made so many good friends on the trail. I was sad to have lost track of them. But the sadness wasn't like the oppressive weight that I felt when Solitaire and Scuba Springsteen left after Port Clinton. This sadness came with a higher perspective. It even came with a smile. I was able to look beyond my own isolation. I knew the sadness was inside me, but it was not significant. The real significance lie outside. I could feel a holy Nothingness that permeated everything: all life and all time. And from that Nothingness we, as individuals, experience a Something: the beautiful, sometimes saddening symphony of events, people, and interactions we call life. I was both a Something and a Nothing, just as all things are. Through the Nothingness, my sadness was acknowledged, but not felt. It became a small skiff of sorrow on the sea of the cosmos. It was too small, too weak to survive the monumental power of the Nothingness that permeates perception. It can survive for a time, but eventually, the skiff shows weakness, falters, and is broken apart in the wholeness of the sea. And all that was, is, and ever will be—all that was not, is not, and never will be—is the Sea.

7-12-13 *8-12-13

Fitzgerald Falls: 1371.5

First full day with the Neil man! His trail name is Joe Don the Megaladon. Sweet name. We did about 13, it was a slow going day. Lots of sharp ascents + descents over glacierized boulders. Fun day, but I think it put a hurting on Neil. He won't be able to pull 20's, but we should be good for 15's. If we can get to Pawling by Friday, I'll consider it a success. 20's are just too long for someone to come out and do for four or five days. Your body just can't handle it. But Neil is trooping through. We're shooting for about 17 tomorrow. We should be good to get that.

Mom + Dad's visit was fun. We resupplied, hung in town for a bit, then did some hiking. They did 2 tough miles out to the shelter, then two back to the car. There was some good rock scrambling in the 2 miles—they did well. And D came out too. Nice surprise. I think she had fun hiking. It was good seeing them—I'm glad they made it out. Well it's a bit after 7pm now. Gonna try for an early start tomorrow morning. So going to call it a night pretty soon. Later!

August 12 Notes: I caught Indy just a few miles before Greenwood Lake. We walked off the trail and waited at an ice cream shop for the arrival of my family and Neil. The ice cream joint was closed, but it overlooked a beautiful low valley. We threw a tennis ball around as cars passed us by every few minutes.

I saw my mother's car turn the corner. My mother, father, sister, and Neil jumped out. Neil is only in his thirties, but he has flecks of silver streaking down his shoulder length hair and his course beard. He looks like a dignified guru of the Eastern arts. He's a good friend of my oldest brother, Matt, the Googan. They went to college together at James Madison University. In the ten years I've known Neil, I've never known him to treat anyone unkindly. Life seems to crash over him, as though he were a boulder in a stream: changing imperceptibly, always there, always dependable. His excitement for the trail was palpable. His pack was heavy, laden with assorted gear like a filter straw and a camp stool. I knew he would have a great experience, I just wasn't sure how he would deal with the physical aspects of hiking. The trail is often not what one believes it to be. After introducing everyone to Indy and loading our things into the car, we headed into town for some food and rest. We got breakfast, resupplied at a general store, then headed over for a swim in Greenwood Lake. I used the swim as my bathing opportunity, only to later find that they had a free shower in the bathroom. I'd be dirty again soon anyway.

After a couple of beers and lunch in town, Mom, Dad, and Danielle hiked a little stretch coming out of Greenwood Lake along with me, Neil, and Indy. There was some fun rock scrambling as we made our way over boulders that had been rubbed smooth by ancient glaciers. At Wildcat Shelter, Indy kept going north. My family and I settled in for a lunch. It would be the last time I would see them on the trail until the end. The distance was now too great for them to make an easy visit. If they were to hike with me again, it would require several days and an airplane ticket. We snacked on our fancy little antipasto—olives, cheese, bread, cured meats, and tomato salad. We passed around a bottle of whiskey, saluting the love of my family, and the sacrifices they undertook to share these moments with me. They signed the shelter log, and I was glad to have my name next to theirs. When there was nothing left to delay our parting, we packed up the remnants of our lunch and prepared to leave. I hugged my mother. I was grateful that she did not cry. It kept me from thinking about what I was leaving. Neil and I turned north. I wrote this journal entry the next night. I would not write the next entry for more than two weeks.

7-26-13 *8-26-13

Home: New Jersey

Lots to catch up on. Let me finish Neil's hiking with me. So as mentioned, the first full day was a little rough. We only did 12 over some tough terrain. But Neil picked it up. The 17 went well. Then I annihilated him with a 22, but to his credit he gutted it out. The best attempted quit occurred midway through the day. He was hiking a few minutes ahead of me. So I came up behind him at a road crossing. And I see him sitting on a guardrail trying to thumb a ride 35 miles into the city. He just said, "Ah man. I was just trying out hitching. If I got a ride I was just going to go into the city + shoot you a text." It was hilarious. But he pushed on. We completed the 22 successfully with a few fairly minor blister issues for Neil. But not bad.

The last day, we pulled about 17 to the shelter a mile before the road to Pawling. Neil survived. He did really well for how many miles I made him do.

He had no idea it was going to be like that. I think the whole thing shocked him. He was posting to Facebook every night about what was going on every day. It was hilarious. I didn't know. I didn't read them until afterward. They were unreal. Sorry, I'm falling asleep over here.

But back to Neil. He hung tough + didn't quit. We made it to the road to Pawling on Friday morning where he attempted (and failed) to hitch into town. He just walked the three or so miles.

Overall, it was great having Neil. After day 1, I thought it was going to be a debacle. But he hung in there and completed his 75 miles or so that he was planning on. Great success.

After leaving Neil, I went on a 5 day tear before hopping off on my 5 day break. Over the 5 day tear, I covered 125 miles to finish up in Dalton, MA.

It was probably the most mileage I've covered in a stretch. The last two days I was zombie-moding pretty good. I also caught back up with Indy during that stretch—just before

Dalton. I saw Bud as well—he got Lyme so was off the trail about 5 days.

Boo Bear + Wash are also pretty much done. They're shuttling to the remaining states, hiking a small section, then moving on. They should be summiting Katahdin soon.

Nothing too exciting happened those 5 days—I was alone most of it. I saw Patches here + there. She was slacking with her parents. I met them—that was nice. They also gave me a ride into Kent. Kent was cool, got dinner there one night.

What else? Some section hikers gave me dehydrated pasta sauce, and pancake mix. The pasta + sauce was awesome —super good. The pancakes on the other hand were a debacle. I tried to make little ones in the bottom of my cup—but failed. I ate lots of raw batter. It was terribly disappointing. And it was after a rough 22 mile day where I wanted more miles but couldn't do it. So that was a rough day + night. At that campsite, I also pooed in a privy that had no box around you, it was just a seat in the middle of the woods. It was hilarious. I thought it was a good joke.

Pulling the average 25's really started to catch up with me. I was very glad for my approaching 5 day break. So on Tuesday night, me + Indy got into Dalton + split a room. We hung + ate at some bar down the road for dinner. It was cool. Dalton was a nice town—a bit more vehicle traffic than I was expecting, but nice.

And after leaving Dalton, my five day break began. It was great. First I drove down to Grandma's for a night. It was good to see her. She did laundry, cooked, we talked. Uncle Mike + Nicky came over. It was a real nice visit. I'm glad I spent time there. She was telling me stories about her + Gramp—ones I never heard. It was great.

Then I headed to Hoboken for a night. I saw John + Laura + the ClearPoint crew.

Then that finally brought me home. I got home Friday.

August 26 Notes: As with most people, the trail wasn't exactly what Neil had imagined. What started as excitement and confidence soon turned into pain, doubt, and confusion. In the end, however, he succeeded in reaching his goal. After five days and 75 miles on the trail, we made it to the road to Pawling, New York. After a final rest at a large tree that stood on the road, we parted ways. Neil made his way toward New York City, and I turned north. He came away from the trip with the feeling that I knew I would have if I ever made it to Katahdin—euphoria for the end of physical exertion, but sadness for the end of a different way of life.

After leaving Neil, the miles piled up behind me. In five days, I'd hike 125 miles: 50 more than I had hiked with Neil. I pushed longer and harder than I had at any point before. My body movements became automatic. I picked my way through the trail without any conscious effort. My mind entered a kind of waking dream state. I thought of nothing consciously. Swimming, nonsensical thoughts would enter the fringes of my conscience, then fade away before I knew what they were.

About ten miles outside of Dalton, I came up behind a hiker. I walked quietly at a distance, trying to figure out who it was. She was middle aged. She had a big, thick afro. She was dirty and she walked with the confident, easy gate of a thru-hiker. But I could tell she was tired. I decided to pass her. I got within about ten feet, and something strange happened: the woman turned into Indy. I hadn't seen him since Wildcat Shelter in New York. *Indy! What is on your head?* He turned and I realized his afro was actually his bug net propped up atop his head. *You look ridiculous!* We hiked into Dalton and split a hotel room that night. In the morning, I got a rental car and drove to my Grandmother's house on Long Island, New York. I caught Indy for one day, then I left him. I hated that.

7-27-13 *8-27-13

Mount Greylock: 1583.0

So continuing on. Got home Friday. Didn't do a ton that day. Did some blogging, showered, hung. I brought Fagan's dog to our home, so I was playing with her. I met Steve Reynolds for dinner at Iron Hill for a farewell meal. He's leaving for California tomorrow actually. Pretty wild. I'm glad I got to see him before he left. Didn't do anything crazy that night. But I did meet up with Leah for ice cream at the farm. It was good to talk to her + meet up.

Saturday was a bit of running around before the wedding. I went to REI to get socks, water treatment drops, and a new knife. Then it was wedding prep time!

The ceremony was nice—at St. John's. Then the party began. It was a blast. Good dancing + hanging. Lou Celli's speech was great. Matt came out as a vampire during his entrance. Overall, it was just a fun time. Then everyone hit Jay's after the reception was done. That place was packed! Steve Olson was there. And I saw Steve Hand too. And Timmy Pearsall I saw for the first time in years. He's a good dude.

Then Sunday was more errands, then a bbq for dinner. Leah came for dinner which I was happy about. It was a fun time, good cap to my 5 days off.

It was a blast being home. I saw a ton of people, ate good food, drank good stuff, and hung.

Jese, I'm falling asleep again. Time to turn in.

August 27 Notes: Along the way to South Jersey, I took some days to visit my Grandmother on Long Island and my good friends in Hoboken. At home, I went to Celli's wedding, hung out with Leah, the beautiful girl I have loved since high school, and saw my college buddy Steve before he moved to California. I saw a lot of people who are very important to me.

But something about the break didn't feel right. I felt dislocated from what I had become. When I started hiking north from Dalton, I had this aching dullness that sat in my chest. It was not regret, and it was not anger, but it was a terrible, cloying angst. By taking that break, I dropped five days behind all my friends. After catching Indy, I immediately left him. After being around Hotshot, Patches, and Bud, I once again fell far behind. The fact that I willingly gave up five hiking days was tough for me to rationalize. Perhaps I made a mistake by taking all those days off. I don't know. Perhaps my angst was due to the fact that I had received a glimpse of the future—the bottomless feeling I would have when my journey was over. Whatever the reason, I second guessed my decision to leave the trail. I still do. I think it's that sometimes I just miss being out on the trail: enjoying the struggle, meeting new people and seeing new things, and living my life unhindered by external pressures. To think that I willingly took a break from a blessing like that is difficult. That's all.

7-28-13 *8-28-13

Campsite: 1601.0

Then it was back on the trail. I left home Monday morning, around 3:30am or something like that. I was back on the trail around 9:30 I think.

The rental car guy who drove me to Dalton was cool. He was a SWCC Boat operator in Cambodia in '68 or so. He told me some neat stories. One, they captured 3 guys and turned them over to the CIA (who came in on a helicopter). The chopper took off, and then out came one of the prisoners. They just pushed him out to get the others talking. He said he was only one of two guys who survived out of his original crew of 5. Then after telling me this, he told me he admired me and other thru hikers. I laughed and told him I admired guys like him. Neat guy—nice dude.

So the past 3 days haven't been too bad. Just still kind of getting back into the swing. I've been doing good miles—sometimes my head isn't all in it though.

And again I'm starting to fall asleep. I need my sleep schedule to get normalized. I need to sleep now. I'm exhausted.

August 28 Notes: Even after hearing about his role in Cambodia, I still saw that man as a "nice dude" and someone to be admired—not because of the actions of his past, but because of his demeanor toward those actions. He sounded detached from his role in the war, as though it were too intense for him to treat as a real event. He liked to talk about it, but it wasn't out of joy or happiness for the things he did. It was simply to share his experiences, both the good and the bad. I'm sure he didn't like seeing a man pushed to his death, but he shared it because it was a part of his life. I don't think the actions of the past make for bad people. It's how we learn from, and eventually overcome those actions that determines who we are.

My fatigue was oppressive at this point on the trail. Even with the five day break, hiking every day all day takes a toll on mental alertness. Once I made camp, I knew I had a limited amount of time and energy before fatigue would set in. I tried to continue writing for as long as I could. But often, I failed to get very far. I would close my journal, cap my pen, and stow them away until the next time I had enough energy and presence of mind to try again.

8-30-13

William B. Douglas Shelter: 1642.0

Nothing much exciting the past two days. I've met a few new people which is cool. This one creepy guy who I think has Tourette's (his name is Bahalana or something like that) told me about a hiker party in Manchester last night. So in order to get to the party, we were supposed to get a ride with Chipmunk's parents from Prospect Rock. But they weren't there when we got there. So that was a little disappointing. I'm kind of glad though. Because Bahalana is weird.

I also met Little Bear + Stretch. They're both cool.

Other than that I'm just hiking. I'm going into Rutland Sunday to do my Fantasy Football draft. So that will be cool to have a hotel/motel room. And I'm trying to figure out how/where I can get to Bahm's. I'm hoping Lyme, NH has a car rental or something.

That just puts me a little further behind my friends. I can't wait 'til there's no more weddings + things to get off the trail for!

I just want to catch my friends and summit Katahdin. Those are my only goals.

I'm going to read a little, then hit the hay. Later.

August 30 Notes: I had entered a large bubble of entirely new hikers. What once felt like a close knit community of thru-hikers now exploded into a rambunctious city that flowed along the trail. At every spring and shelter, I met a new face. Gone was the chance meeting of a hiker who turned out to be a friend of a friend—someone you felt you already knew through the stories of others. Those meetings were replaced by guarded conversations in which each side attempted to determine the legitimacy of the other. They often ended with a failed search for information: *Have you seen Patches, Hotshot, or Indy?* They would squish their faces. They'd shake their head. *No. I never met any of them, sorry.* It was an odd feeling of displacement, almost as if I was starting the trail over again—meeting new people and sorting out my place amongst them.

I was different from many of the people in this bubble, and I felt it. Many in the bubble had been hiking a longer time than I. They often started their northbound thru-hike in March or April. I started in May. They were relaxed, laid back, lacking any sense of urgency. They were just hiking, and whether they made it to the end didn't much matter. It wasn't a bad thing. Secretly, I often envied them for their ways. Although I hiked more deliberately than many of them, I was not necessarily a faster or better hiker. Obviously I moved more quickly through the southern portion of the trail, but by this point, anyone still on the trail was an excellent hiker. It was not our physical differences that set us apart, but our demeanors and our outlooks on the trail. I felt a sense of mission, both in catching my friends and in completing my thru-hike. But what I saw as a sense of mission, they saw as frivolous energy. In their eyes, my most defining characteristic was the fact that I began my thru-hike in May. I was tagged with the playfully disparaging label of *Mayfly*: a thru-hiker who started in the month of May, and by implication, a thru-hiker who moved too fast, hiked too hard, and didn't take it all in.

Despite the differences in our thru-hiking philosophies,

114

I became friends with a lot of good people in this bubble—hikers like Mailman, Uke, Lost and Found, Smiley, Dr. Suess, and MacGyver. They were a different crowd than what I was used to, but their jovial attitude and welcoming smiles made it hard to dislike them. But even in their good natured company, I lacked the presence of great friends. I missed the bond I had with Munchies and Tangy down south, and then with Patches, Indy, and Hotshot through the middle states. But as I neared the Whites and the most challenging portion of the trail, I stumbled across several friends, both old and new, that would be with me until the end.

Note: The dates are correct from this point forward. I would not write an entry until September 10. As has happened in previous entries, my failure to record entries more frequently results in my next entry being disjointed. There are a number of events recorded out of order and many are mentioned only briefly.

9-10-13

Liberty Spring Campsite: 1815.5

Haven't written in a while. It's been kind of crazy in this mad dash to October 15. I'll recount what I can, hopefully all the highlights.

So luckily, I left Bahalana behind, he creeped me out a bit. The crowd I've been around now mostly is Scratch + Trucker. Then I also kind of ran into a bubble consisting of a lot of names I heard before. Like Lost + Found, Smiley, Uke. Then I've also met some others in that crew like Mailman, Whisper, AO, River, + some others—including Hail Satan who I'm not a big fan of. He's a THer big time. Everyone else is cool though.

So let's see—what's happened? A couple days after passing Manchester, I went into Rutland for 2 days. The first night I stayed at the Yellow Deli + saw Munchies for the first time since Hot Springs, NC. He's somewhere around me right now. But the Yellow Deli was a cool hostel. It's run by a religious community called the Twelve Tribes who are really super nice. You get an awesome breakfast in the morn. And it's just a neat place. They invited me to a Sabbath dinner, but by the time I got showered up I was a little late, so I didn't go. Munchies went the night before + said it was neat—weird, but an experience. So it was an interesting place, but pretty cool.

The second night in Rutland I got a hotel room so I could have some privacy during my fantasy draft. Brother Matt helped me out with the draft, doing all the stuff on the site + giving me tips (I haven't followed much news obviously). My team turned out pretty good—I crushed Sean this past week. So that was a good zero in Rutland. But the next morning sucked. I couldn't get a hitch to the trail—I walked about 7 miles down the road. Some dude picked me up a half mile from the trailhead. Nice, but at that point not worth it. So that sucked.

I should have hopped the train that was passing by as I left town. I think it went right to the trailhead. Would have been scary, but probably worth it. That walk sucked, but oh well.

That night though I stayed at the Lookout, this cool cabin with a lookout perch on top. I drafted through Paul for our Son of SYN league up there. It was awesome. I was the only one at the cabin. My bad, I actually stayed there a few days after Rutland.

Right after Rutland, I stayed at the Long Trail Inn. Cool little hotel/lodge with a legit pub. The pub was great. Good food + good beers. Wood Elf + Poncho were there. They both split off there though because they're hiking the Long Trail. Both were cool guys. Poncho I saw on + off for about a week prior. He looked like John Goodman.

I first met Wood Elf atop a mountain a few days before. There was a conversation he + a few guys had for a while that I kind of just chilled + listened to. One of the guys packed beers up there, so I had a couple.

But anyway, the Long Trail Inn was a good stop. Paul + Ma sent me a package there too. That was awesome. Next highlight was getting into Hanover. I only spent a few hours there, but it was a cool town. I got some food, hung out, nothing special. But it was nice. I gave Bahm a call there too to tell him I couldn't make the wedding. I was struggling over that decision for days before. I wish I could have made it. But I'm just getting too close to the end. He understood. That was the first time I talked to him like that in a while. He's a good dude. I need to hang with him more.

Then leaving Hanover, I had a couple normal days before I hit the Whites. Right before the start of the Whites (Mount Moosilake) I stayed the night at Hiker's Welcome hostel. A bunch of people were there (like 20) which was weird but cool. The hostel was decent. Caretaker was weird. Probably wouldn't stay there again—but it was a decent break. Drank a few beers and watched a couple movies. But I forgot two days before that, I spent a few hours at Bill Ackerly's house. He's just some old guy who lets hikers come hang at his house. Nice old man. I played a game of croquet with him + 2 others. The game ended when about 10 other hikers rolled up (Uke, Mailman, Lost + Found, Smiley, etc). Neat place though, and Bill was a neat guy.

Another cool thing happened about 2 miles before Bill's. Cannon + Lady got engaged up on the mountain. It was funny because I was the first one to come across them after the engagement (about 30 min after). I could tell something was weird when I came up. And after an awkward minute, they told me they were engaged. It was pretty awesome. They were both super excited. Then down at Bill's, Bill broke out a pound cake + we ate that in celebration. I got to take pictures of the festivities with Cannon's awesome camera. So I was a pretty big player in their engagement! It was pretty funny. Neat stuff though!

So that's all the big stuff leading up to the Whites. I'm a couple days into the Whites, and they are tough! Gonna stop writing now and sleep. But will write soon. Things to write about so far in the Whites: Scratch's backstory; the difficulty; Scratch's trail magic; the lodges.

September 10 Notes: The date of October 15—the unofficial deadline for summiting Katahdin—hung over my head. It became a frequent, yet uneasy topic of conversation along the trail: *Do you think you can make it to Katahdin before the fifteenth?* If I could not make the deadline, my contingency plan was to flip flop. But to be so close and to have to flip flop didn't seem right. So I set my mind to making it. I planned on reaching Katahdin Stream Campground, the base of Mount Katahdin, at least several days before the fifteenth. Now, with only a month to go and over 400 miles of trail remaining, I had to make it a reality. To be clear, summiting after the fifteenth is not impossible; however, it can be very treacherous and is often not allowed due to path closures and bad weather. Even in the early weeks of October, weather can get bad enough that nobody is allowed up Katahdin. I had learned that weather can change rapidly and drastically, especially at altitude, so I needed to give myself a buffer of several days to take into account any inclement weather that may be rolling through central Maine in early to mid October. The looming immediacy of the deadline added further purpose to my sense of mission. I continued to hike hard and strong as I moved through New England.

My memories of Massachusetts are somewhat few and far between: I hiked often with Indy, I saw Bahalana defecating only feet from the trail, and I first met a guy who would later become a good friend. Just north of the MA/VT border, I ran across a hiker who looked like he was in a world of pain. I was at the end of my hiking day with only a mile to go. I just had to summit a small hill, then drop down to a stream on the other side and make camp. The man was about thirty with short brown hair that was balding slightly at the top. He had big blue eyes, and a short, well trimmed beard. He didn't have the emaciated look of a thru-hiker—he was strong and broad. *Hey, how're ya?* He was sitting on a log, massaging his knee. *Good, you? You hurting?* He smiled up grimly. *Just a little achy. Just kind of getting back into the swing of things again.* It was one of his first days back on the trail after an injury. *I was at a trail angel's in Dalton— sleeping on a couch in their living room. I got up in the night to piss, it was pitch black. So I stand up, and I take my first step, and hit my foot on the coffee table.* He sprained his toes badly. They swelled and bruised. He eventually went home, resting up for a month before he was able to return to the trail. Atop the hill, he was

118

thinking of calling it a day—his knee was achy and he just didn't have the energy to go on. There was a nice camp site there, but no water. *Let me see how much I got. I just filled up a bit back. Here, I can give you this half liter.* I held up my small Nalgene water bottle. *And I can give you like a liter here.* I showed him what remained in my water bladder. *You want it?* He hesitated. *Well, where are you going tonight?* He was worried that I wouldn't have enough water for myself. *I'm just headed down the hill here. There's a stream down there. I'll just fill up there.* He accepted the water and thanked me. I hiked on, thinking that I'd never see him again. He was exhausted, gimpy, and just coming back from a month long break. There was no way he could hike well. A week later, as a thunderstorm rolled through a shelter in the mountains of Vermont, I saw Trucker again. He introduced me to a buddy—Scratch. I had found new friends.

And I found some old friends too. As I walked into the common room at the Yellow Deli in Rutland, I saw Munchies. We were only in Rutland for one night together. It felt like the early days of the trail. We went to the bar, ate a bunch of food, and laughed about nothing special. The only thing missing was Tangy. Munchies hiked out of Rutland on my zero. But I would soon catch him and we would hike a lot of the remainder of the trail together. Soon after Rutland, I caught back up with Indy, and I began to settle into a loosely cohesive group consisting of my old friends Indy and Munchies, and my new friends, Trucker and Scratch.

A couple of days later, I made my way down to the Long Trail Inn, a landmark that sits just off the spot where the Vermont Long Trail breaks off from the AT. I went down for just a beer, a meal, and to pick up a maildrop, but I wound up spending the night. The package was a bit late in getting there, and I couldn't leave it behind. I was glad to have an excuse for a relaxing night of beers and food. I spent most of my time at the bar, sampling assorted foods and local beers. Poncho and Wood Elf kept me company for part of the day, and during the rest, I did laundry and got cleaned up. The next morning, I awaited the arrival of my maildrop. I stood outside until the mail truck arrived, walked inside with the delivery man, and then immediately signed off for it from the Inn. Inside was an assortment of goodies and a black and white picture of my brother Solitaire's creepy face with a note scribbled on the back. I packed up my food bag, slipped the note into my journal, and set out toward Hanover, New Hampshire.

From Hanover, I had planned on leaving the trail one last time. My childhood friend was getting married, and a celebration was planned in South Jersey. Over the previous couple of weeks, I wrestled with the decision to leave the trail again in order to make it there. In the end, I decided not to go. I called Kyle and told him I would not make it. I went to the store to get a pair of gloves, one of the cold weather essentials I lacked, and hiked out of town. As I left Hanover, I felt the tension between my two seemingly disparate lives—home and trail. I wanted to be home and to experience every moment with all my friends and family. But I also wanted to hike forever and experience all the good things there are to see in the world. I wanted to be free. I hiked into the woods, away from the cars, the cell phones, the stores, the obligations of the modern world. The earth grew soft, the trail took me in.

The next day, as I crossed a road and rounded a bend in the trail, I came upon an odd sign. It was hand painted: the face of an old man surrounded by ice cream and water. I was unsure of whether or not to take up this strange old man on his offer of "free ice cream," and "free water." I wanted to get moving on down the trail. I still had over ten miles to Hexacuba Shelter. I stared up the AT, then turned off and made my way down a short trail through some shrubs towards the home of Bill Ackerly. I approached the house slowly. I didn't hear anyone or see any movement. I stepped up to the door and before I could rap my knuckles on the frame of the screen, an old man with tufts of white hair came sliding into view. Bill Ackerly welcomed me in as though I were a grandson. He sat me down in a chair, introduced me to two other hikers who were sitting at the kitchen table, got me some ice cream, and immediately drew me into the conversation he was having with the young woman. Bill told us stories about Pete Seeger, an old folk musician and activist. He then reminisced about his earlier days as a Trail Angel, when he welcomed hikers into his home for reasons he couldn't quite explain. After showing me to the coolers set out by some other Trail Angels, he challenged us to a game of croquet. I grabbed a beer from the cooler and followed him outside. He was a man who moved without the weight of his age upon him. He swung the mallet fluidly. He helped the girl when she asked what to do next, and he laughed at every opportunity. With me and Bill battling for the top spot as we moved into the last few wickets, a crowd of hikers, including Trucker, Mailman, Smiley, Uke, and Lost and Found appeared on Bill's porch. Smiley's dog sprinted toward the game. She picked up a croquet ball, ran several yards, then dropped it. She proceeded to do that to each ball. Bill graciously called the game a draw. The gathering soon turned into an engagement celebration with the arrival of Cannon and Lady. After cake, beers, and pictures, I pried myself away from the magical little abode of Bill Ackerly. I saddled my pack, looked around at the goodness that the trail had to offer, and approached Bill. *Thank you. This was fun. I appreciate it a ton.* Trucker slung on his pack as well and we hit the trail. As I walked, I realized why I was so grateful to Bill Ackerly. What I wish I thanked him for was his acceptance of me, for treating me as a person with thoughts and ideas of my own, for sharing his past and his ideas with me, and for being the pinnacle of the spirit of the trail. I hiked toward Hexacuba Shelter with Trucker. We made camp, and after dinner, I overheard Hail Satan talking to Trucker. Hail Satan was a brash kid who only had one topic of conversation: the merits of atheism and the failures of religion. He said he also went by the trail name Beelzebub. But for all his theories of religion, he didn't even know who Beelzebub was. He was long and thin, and he only wore black. After the lightness of Bill Ackerly's home, the woods seemed heavy with Hail Satan in them.

At the foot of Mount Moosilake, the gateway to the Whites, stands a hiker hostel, Hikers Welcome. It is a fairly standard hostel—bunks, shuttles, snacks, and showers. There were a lot of hikers who stayed there with me that night. I was still very much in the bubble that I entered in New York. I spent the night in an outdoor bunkhouse, which was just a large, insulated tent. For the first time on my trip, I began to feel the biting chill that I would encounter over the final month of my journey. I woke up early and immediately put on every item of clothing I had. I made my way to the hiker box and pulled out a green winter hat. It was much too small—it barely came down around my ears, but I needed it. I ate a breakfast of pancakes and bacon. Then I left Hikers Welcome. I was happy to be free of the crowd at the hostel. I was happy to be free from the caretaker, a man who had a lot in common with Hail Satan. I hiked out a bit after Scratch and Trucker and caught them on the summit of Moosilake. I finally entered the area that had been talked about in awe—The White Mountain National Forest, home of the presidential range and the most difficult stretch of trail on the AT.

9-22-13

Campsite: 1942.5

Had to get a new journal. Ran out of pages in the original. It's weird writing in this one. It's much nicer.

Right now I don't feel great. I'm missing home a bit and just want to get done with this trip. Paul left earlier today. It's always tough when someone visits or you go home. It's tough to get focused on the trail again. It was great having Paul out though—lots of fun. It just makes me miss home though.

I just put a rough plan together for the rest of the trip. Looks like I'll finish up right around the 10th or before. Before would be ideal. It's pretty weird to be planning for the end, even if it is preliminary planning. It's strange. It will be bittersweet. I'm ready for it to end, but I don't want to leave the trail. This trip has been such a mental game. I always tell people it's all mental. And when morale is low, it's rough.

I just don't know what I want. In some ways, I've figured things out, but I still am so confused about life, both mine + in general. I'm kind of scared for the future. This dread comes over me sometimes. Like it did before the trail as well. I think it's just part of who I am. I know there's so much to be excited + happy about, but sometimes I just can't shake this damn dread.

Maybe I just need sleep + stuff. Anyway, need to write about: Scratch, the Huts, finishing the Whites, Paul's trip Part Deux, The Cabin. I'll write again tonight.

September 22 Notes: My sporadic journal entries became nonexistent as I hiked through the Whites. My original journal was a spiral notebook. I used it as a dual purpose notebook: the front being used for planning and the back being used for journaling. Just before the Whites, I realized that I was out of pages as my planning section and journaling section met. I had to get out of the Whites and into Gorham, New Hampshire before I was able to purchase a new journal. Even then, it took me several days to start writing in it. During the twelve day writing hiatus, I had gone through the Whites, met up with an old coworker of mine at Pinkham Notch, taken a zero in Gorham and saw Bud for the last time, hiked with my brother Paul, and entered the final leg of my journey, moving to within 250 miles of Katahdin.

In the mayhem of my final weeks on the trail, many details were omitted from my journal, especially with regard to my initial movements through the Whites. The Whites, in their majesty, size, and treachery were like nothing I had seen on the trail. In the following journal entries, several events that occurred in the Whites are recorded, but many are not. I failed to describe some of the most beautiful sights and some of the most desperate times. I will attempt to make up for that now. On my first day in the Whites, I completed seventeen miles with relative ease, summiting Moosilake and finishing the day at Eliza Brook Shelter. I felt that the Whites had been overhyped. I had heard many warnings about them, but I still felt that I could easily complete nearly twenty miles per day.

The second day, I moved up and over the peaks of Kinsman Mountain and passed by Lincoln, New Hampshire, confident that I could push on without a full resupply in town. I approached Franconia Ridge. Never in my life have I seen anything like that image of Lafayette Mountain. It grew out of the earth, a blade destroying the sphere of the world. The sun was bright. The winds tore around me, shuttering my ears. I reached the top of Lafayette, and I felt as though that pinnacle of earth was one of the universe's greatest creations—a place from which I could both feel myself, gazing outward, and forget myself entirely, absorbed in the manifestation of the cosmos. I moved onward through the Whites, making camp that night in the woods just short of Zealand Falls Hut. A storm ripped through the darkness and the rains fell. I woke with a heavy dampness on the floor, and my sleeping pad heavily moist.

I hiked nearly fifteen miles the next day through lower altitudes, completing my day at Mizpah Spring Hut, close to the approach to Mount Washington. That evening, right after setting up tent, another storm rolled through out of nowhere. What was once sunny, blue sky quickly turned a frightening grey. The next morning, I packed up early in preparation for my ascent of Mount Washington, perhaps the most perilous mountain on the entire AT. Every year, there are ill-prepared hikers who never come off the mountain. Weather changes drastically at an altitude of 6,288 feet. As I began my hike up Washington, the weather was perfect. Throughout the morning, I moved quickly, excited to reach the top and to eat lunch. I knew there was a structure at the top of the mountain, but I wasn't sure exactly what to expect. When I rounded the last bend, I found not just one structure, but several. One looked like some kind of power facility, another was a small building that I did not go into, and the third was a cafeteria and the cog train stop—a railway that ferries tourists up and down the mountain. The top of the mountain was not as serene as I thought it would be. But I was glad to have a cafeteria. I headed inside and consumed a hearty meal. I also got some cellular service at the top, so I spent an hour or so texting my old friend, Cindy, who lived in the New England area. We were trying to find a place and a time to meet up. I lost reception. I looked outside. Clouds began to move in. Blue skies turned into fog and rain. Two hikers, gnarled, overweight hippies, told me their plan: they would take the cog train down to town and stay there the night. Then they would train back up the next day and resume their hike from there. I listened to their plan, but never gave it serious consideration. There was no way I was going to take a train off Washington. As the cog train was making its slow climb back up the mountain, I slipped on my gloves, hat, and rain gear. The crowd of people stood like cattle, jamming the door of the cafeteria and spilling out onto the platform. I slipped through them, ignoring the few faces that understood what I was doing. I was moving out into the grey, toward the treacherous descent of the mountain by foot.

My plan was to get below the storm by making it to Osgood Tent Site, less than ten miles from Mount Washington and almost 4,000 feet lower. But I barely even made it to Mad Hause—Madison Spring Hut, only 5.7 miles from Washington. The naked rocks were slick. I fell several times. I hiked for six hours. And for the first time, I was afraid about what could happen to me. After the first couple of hours, I began to shiver as the wetness seeped through my cheap rain jacket and clung to my skin. I shivered and struggled through the final miles. My hands, cold inside the thin gloves, stayed rigid around my trekking poles. I did not stop to check my trail guide or to eat. It was too cold to do anything besides walk. My head stayed down, carefully picking each spot to place a foot. I looked up only to search for the cairns that marked the path of the trail. Above treeline, the white blazed trees that had marked most of the trail gave way to small monoliths of stone called cairns. Many hours into my descent, I still hadn't seen any other hikers on the trail. And I didn't know how far I was from Madison Spring Hut. I lifted my head to check for cairns and saw two dark shapes in front of me. I approached the two hikers. *Hey. How're you guys doing?* They turned and stood off the trail to let me pass. *Good. Wet and cold. But ok. You going to Madison Hut?* The man had a thick beard. *Yeah, I can't make it any further than that.* It was too wet and cold to say much more. Sometime later, I walked into Madison Spring Hut. I dropped my things and changed into my dry clothes, secured safely within my pack.

The young couple I had passed on the trail came in about fifteen minutes later. Their names were Sweets and Grits. I also met Coon, Slim, Fire Hydrant, and Caveman. Besides us, there were about forty other, non thru-hikers staying at the hut. As payment for our free stay at the hut (thru-hikers are often granted work for stay options at the Appalachian Mountain Club Huts), we held a question and answer session with the non thru-hikers after dinner. I assumed it would be quick and boring. But instead of a quiet room of people wanting to get back to their bunks to spend some time alone, we were encircled by the whole crowd as they threw out questions: *What do you do with dirty clothes? Where do you get food? What made you do this? What did you do before the trail? Have you been scared? Has your gear stood up to the miles? Has your mother been scared?* All I could see were smiles and slacked jaws of awe. Strangers, complete strangers, saw me as a thru-hiker, someone who bucked the assumed obligations of life to do something different. They were confident in me and proud of what I had done—not just because I had 300 miles to go, but because I had begun to walk in the first place. I could have talked all night, but the lodgers soon moved off to their bunk rooms. We thru-hikers shifted the dining room furniture, settling in to sleep atop the tables and benches.

The next morning, I ate breakfast and swept out the bunk rooms—my final work for stay task at Madison Hut. I pulled on my still soaked clothes and walked into the misty rain that had not relented in the night. I made the short hike up and over Mount Madison, and finally began my descent out of the +5,000 foot mountains. The trip down Madison was long, slow, and difficult. After several hours, I finally dropped down to around 2,500 feet and passed by Osgood Tent Site, the place I had hoped to reach the night before. With my clothes still soaking wet, and in need of rest from my descents of Washington and Madison, I took up my former coworker Cindy on an offer of a meal and a place to stay. I reached Pinkham Notch, and within a couple of hours, I saw Cindy and her fiance Rick pull up with their camper in tow. I climbed in and we made our way to a campsite down the road. After six whole days in the Whites, I was not yet done. I still had to make my way across 21 more miles. And I had another task, one more difficult even than the Whites: I still had to come to terms with the fact that this trip would soon end. And with its end, I would return to the "real world" and the sense of dread that accompanied it. I was scared that what I had become would be wiped away by what I would become. I had become me. I did not want to become anything else. But at least, for one night, I had some friends, a bed in a camper, and a glass of whiskey in my hand.

9-24-13

Perham Stream: 1980.8

I fell asleep real early the other night, so didn't write again. I have a lot to recount, I'll do my best. I'm taking a zero the day after tomorrow so may leave some writing for then.

So let's see. Let's start with the fact that I finished the Whites a while ago! But the hard stuff certainly is not done yet. Today was rough, but I'll get to that. Finishing the Whites was awesome though. It was a big psychological hurdle to complete. They were all they were made up to be. They were hard as hell. I'm not sure if I wrote about Cindy's visit. But after the brutality that was the descent of Washington, and then more rain coming off Madison (tough descent as well), I took Cindy up on her offer to meet at Pinkham Notch and spend a night in the camper. Her + Rick came up. It was an awesome visit, I truly needed it. They picked me up in the Notch around 7 and we went to a campsite down the road. We just hung, drank, ate, talked a lot. Rick is a cool guy. It was good to meet him. As I'm writing this, I think I may have already written about it. But oh well. It was a great break from the Whites. I'm glad they came out.

Then the next day, I went up Wildcat and then spent the night in a hut at Carter Notch. It was cool because there were no guests there, just 5 or so thru hikers. So we just kind of hung with the crew, they made us an awesome pot sticker dinner. And in the morning we ate sausage + coffee + some weird baked oatmeal thing—but mostly sausage. I think I had like 10 sausage patties. The work wasn't bad. At night we wiped down the walls of the common room and in the morn we just wiped down our bunk room's baseboards + swept. Easy work for a free stay. Dimples, Fire Hydrant, Caveman, + Grits + Sweets were there. Grits + Sweets are cool—I've enjoyed hanging with them here + there the past couple of weeks. But I think I'm far up on them now. Probably won't see them again.

The next day, I left Carter Notch + hiked out of the Whites! I finished my day at White Mountain Hostel just outside of Gorham. Cool + super nice place. Ate some free leftovers for dinner, then ate some Ben + Jerry's while watching the Gladiator. It was a good night! Met a bunch of new faces there which is weird at this stage. Most of them were a little strange. Wooden Spoon, Willow, Stealth + some others were there. The only one I really know well there was Trucker. But it was a good night + a good sleep.

Two old section hikers were there. I've never heard two guys talk more about how we won't reach Katahdin in time. It was amazing. Their room was next to mine, only separated by a curtain. And I could hear their whole conversation as they prepped for bed. It was all about how hard the trail was coming up, and how we're a "day late and a dollar short"— their words. It was funny.

Breakfast was awesome in the morn—some weird creme brule french toast or something like that. Then it was back on the trail to get to my meet up point with Paul.

It was a decent few days to Grafton Notch. A few interesting things happened though.

I lost Trucker but found Scratch. I still need to write about Scratch—but not now.

I went through the Mahoosic Notch. It was pretty awesome. It's about a mile of really fun, but potentially dangerous boulder hopping. Lots of sliding + jumping + lowering. Poles are worthless there. It took me an hour + 20 minutes to finish it. It was pretty neat, but I got a couple little holes in the bottom of my pack from it. Definitely one of the more memorable stretches of the trail though. Then it was out of the Notch and up Mahoosic Arm. Overall, the day was pretty rough. But I did about 18 to get to Grafton Notch to meet Paul in the morning, so I was happy about that! I'll get to

Paul's trip though.

The last interesting thing that happened in that stretch was with Cannon and Lady. Apparently they got in a big fight at Carlo Col Shelter and Lady left in the middle of the night. So in the morning, I saw Cannon and he asked if he could hike with me to reach the road so he could get into Andover and find Lady. It was pretty bizarre. At that point I knew nothing about the fight or anything so I was confused. So he set out a couple minutes before me since he was sick + going slowly. I told him I'd catch up in a few. So when I did hit the trail, about a half mile in, I see him + Lady standing there, Lady crying her eyes out. So I never got the whole story from Cannon. I got most of it through Scratch actually. But either way, Lady is back + they are all good!

Anyway, I'm going to turn in. Still need to write about: Scratch's story, Paul's trip, the weather, Saddleback Mtn, and I think that's it. Here's to hoping for some better weather tomorrow + making it into Stratton at a decent time! Night.

September 24 Notes: Following my night with Cindy and Rick, I took a zero in Gorham. I still wasn't ready to put my pack on and finish out the Whites. Cindy and Rick's hospitality and company were great, and I couldn't pull myself away from town life just yet. I resupplied and spent the night at a hostel called The Barn. I saw Bud for the last time—he would be skipping ahead to Kathadin before heading home to Tennessee. He had some things he had to attend to that he could not push off. After a couple of beers together, we wished each other well and that was it.

I walked alone down Main Street as the sun set over the hills surrounding Gorham. I was glad to have a bed waiting for me at the hostel. I walked upstairs to the bunk room to find two older section hikers and a middle aged man with thick glasses. My conversation with the older hikers was quietly interrupted by murmurs. The man with the thick glasses was repeating bible verses to himself under his breath. Over the next hour, the verses turned into violent rants about a number of seemingly unrelated topics: the Great Recession, the blight and threat of immigration, the death of American morality, and the need for true followers of God. All was justified, piously and poisonously, with bible verses that he spit from memory. He was not a hiker, but a traveling vagabond walking the streets from south to north while spreading his mentally ill gospel of hate, paranoia, and fear. In the second floor bunk room, I rolled out my sleeping bag on the bed. *Do you guys carry knives on the trail?* The two older hikers remained quiet. I walked across the room toward the staircase. *Just a little penknife,* I said. *For cutting open food packaging and things.* This was a lie. I didn't want to bring up my three-inch folding blade for fear of what he would say. His eyes narrowed behind the thick glasses, magnifying the slits. *Oh, well that's no fun.* He looked away, lost in thought. *Well, do you ever skin any animals on the trail?* I walked past him and placed my first foot on the steps. *No.* I walked outside to find refuge from his mind. I called home. My hopes for a quiet sleep in a soft bed soon turned to thoughts of how I could protect myself in the night. I slept with my knife and my headlamp in my hands. In the middle of the night, I woke to the man walking around the bunk room. He was wandering back and forth across the floor. Then he went downstairs. I heard him rummage around for a while before returning to the bunk room. That sequence of events happened several times throughout the night. I held my knife and headlamp closely. I woke up early, around 6am, and left.

I hitched a ride out of town after updating my blog. I hiked up and over the Wildcats and spent the night at Carter Notch. I slept easily that night in my own bunkroom, comforted by the knowledge that those around me—Dimples, Caveman, Fire Hydrant, Sweets, and Grits—were all of sane mind. I was around this group for a few days as we moved through the last stage of the Whites. Dimples, whose smile left nearly permanent dimples in her face, was a middle aged woman, very petite and energetic. Caveman and Fire Hydrant were tight with each other, but they had a love hate relationship a lot of the time. They talked a lot, but at least most of what they said was funny. Sweets and Grits exuded southern charm and kindness. They were very humble and kind people. They were finishing their hike from the previous year. Sweets had fallen and busted a few ribs in the Whites, cutting their thru-hike short. For how sweet and proper she looked, she was one of the toughest girls I met out there. Throughout the Whites, I saw her hike through some of the most brutal weather I encountered, all without hesitation or a word of negativity.

The fight between Cannon and Lady was something that came and passed quickly. I believe it was a direct result of the physically demanding nature of the trail during this stretch. The day in and day out physical and psychological rigor of long distance hiking was taking a toll on our morale, whether we knew it or not. In this instance, those effects led to a fight between two people who love each other. There were many difficult points on the trail, but one of the toughest was four days after leaving Carlo Col Shelter. I went over Saddleback Mountain. The mountain itself is not overly imposing: about a 1,500 foot climb to an elevation of 4,120 feet over 2.3 miles. It is big, but it is not anything we hadn't done before. It is a tall mountain though, getting up above treeline for quite some time. On the day I summited, the clouds that crowned the top of Saddleback brought a mixture of freezing rain, sleet, and other wintry precipitation. I broke treeline, and immediately was thrown into the white washed world of the wintery storm. My rain jacket was no match for the moisture and wind. I was immediately soaked outside and in. Without trees to hinder the wind, every bit of body heat was whisked away into the white clouds. Signposts were frozen over in windswept icicles. I was getting dangerously cold—even colder than I had been on Washington. I   broke into a run across the top of the mountain. My trekking poles clinked across the hard rock and my feet went numb. After about a half hour of running, climbing, and scrambling, I finally dropped below treeline and out of the warmth sucking winds. I removed my hood and my bandana from my face, and continued downward, intent on reaching a warmer altitude. I heard talking on the trail ahead. Cannon and Lady were recovering from the ordeal of Saddleback. They had been right in front of me the whole time. Cannon silently hugged Lady as she shivered. *No woman should ever have to do that! That was horrible, it was terrible!* Lady, with Cannon by her side, released the frustrations and fears that were pent up inside of all of us. The trail demanded things of us. And we were scared, I was scared. The physical and psychological demands of the journey were taking their toll.

9-26

Safford Notch Campsite: 2008.1

Lost my pen, so need to write with this Sharpie for now. Did not zero in Stratton today, so did not catch up on writing. Left town around 2:30pm and hiked 10 miles into the dark. So it was a late hiking day. Hoping to get done a little earlier tomorrow so I can do some writing. It is going to be a pain though with this Sharpie!

Turning in now. That was probably my last night hike of the trip—and I'm happy about that!

Zach had his baby today. Super cute. Pretty cool stuff.

Night.

September 26 Notes: The previous day, I hitched a ride into Stratton. I walked to the general store for a resupply and to the laundromat. While my clothes turned in the machine, I texted Indy, Hotshot, and Patches. They were only a couple of days ahead. I picked up my resupply and my clean clothes and walked to the hostel. I planned out the rest of my trip, day by day and mile by mile. I capped my pen and walked to Munchies' room. We cracked a beer and watched television. My new plan required me to leave Stratton without a zero. I would summit Katahdin on October 6, 2013.

9-27

Pierce Pond Lean-to: 2030.7

Found my pen! Unfortunately it's pretty late already. Got to camp about 6:30. Just got in my tent after 8:00 and I'm exhausted. Did about 23 miles or so—it was a drain.

Shooting for another long day tomorrow so I can get into Monson at a decent hour. I have a lot to catch up on with writing—hope to do it soon. I'm just too drained right now to do it. I'm falling asleep. Night.

September 27 Notes: My trail life was slow to reach paper. I still had a lot of events to record. Each night that I fell asleep without writing, I felt the burden grow heavier. I knew my memory would shift and alter. So I needed the journal—a piece of the present made eternal. The written word may only be a set of cultural symbols, yet it pulls at something deeper than the ink marks.

With my daily distance decided for the rest of the trip, I felt the end. Everything I had been doing for the past five months: each step I took, each entry I recorded, each person I met, was all part of a culmination that would occur in the next ten days. I was afraid to think about it, I was afraid to be done with my life on the trail. I wished I could turn back time and do it all again.

9-28

Moxie Bald Mountain Lean-to: 2053.5

Long 24 mile day. Waking at 3am tomorrow to get into town. Will write when I can.

September 28 Notes: The trail demands something of each individual who walks it. What we are bleeds into the earth. What the earth is bleeds back into us. What appears as two disparate entities is a manifestation of a single existence. The demands of the trail are my own demands: to hike, to learn, to realize the paradox of existence. I am compelled to accept those demands because they are reciprocal.

But the demands of the world outside of the trail are not my own. Why can't the world demand of me something greater than money, title, possession? Why can't it demand that I discover myself? Why can't it demand something higher? I was afraid to leave the trail because I didn't understand the demands of the outside world. I was afraid of my future.

9-30

Long Pond Stream Lean-to: 2086.5

I'll write some tonight although not all. I left Monson this morning and got 15 in. I'm about 100 miles from Katahdin!

Let me write about Scratch first. Back near the Whites + a bit before, I met Scratch. He's good buddies with Trucker. He's a cool, normal, middle aged guy. So when he told me his backstory, I was shocked. Apparently, he was addicted to crack in his earlier years. He lived a kind of double life—had a job in IT, went to church, normal stuff. But every once in a while he would go on a raging alcohol + crack fueled bender. He would drink, then go to the crack house and get crazy. So he no longer drinks at all.

One day he wrote a letter to his roommate asking for help, left it out for him, and went to sleep. He got in AA and stuff and he's good now. Unfortunately, his IT career is over because of background checks when he was contracting with the government. He hasn't worked in IT since then. He just kind of does odd jobs now. Good dude, but I feel a little bad for him. Good work by him though to change his life. He's a good guy.

Anyway, I hiked with him + Trucker through a lot of the Whites. But I probably won't see either of them again.

Last I saw them was about a week ago when Paul came to visit.

Paul's visit was awesome. We met at the Notch as planned. Although when I first got to the lot I was upset because I didn't think he was there. I saw no cars that looked like rentals. Then out of nowhere, he popped out of a nice Jeep Liberty. It was funny. So we hiked about ten that first day. We camped at an awesome little campsite on a stream. We chilled, cooked dinner (I had my first ever MRE), and then hit the hay. Nothing special but it was a fun time.

I need to sleep—I'm passing out. Will write/continue tomorrow hopefully.

To write about: Paul's trip, the Cabin, the weather, Stratton, Tangy, Monson, the Lakeshore House.

September 30 Notes: Scratch was small, but he carried his large pack well. He was around forty, and had short dark hair and a groomed goatee with flecks of silver peaking through. He had a slight accent that I couldn't place, but I think it was a little bit New England. His image betrayed no evidence of his past. He was bright, well groomed, and a smile always creased his face.

I removed a short paragraph describing some of his life in the entry above as the details were not fully accurate. Suffice it to say, Scratch's past was a nightmarish collage of drugs and violence. Before I knew he was a recovering addict, I offered him beers every once in a while. He always politely declined: *Maybe one day. But I can't do it now.* Through him, I gained insight into a darkness that I have never fought. All hikers have a story —I am honored that Scratch shared his with me.

10-1

Carl A. Newhall Lean-to: 2107.3

First day of October! And the end is close. So weird. Pulled a 21 miler or so today. Was pretty rough. Got in a few minutes after dark. Tomorrow is the last day of any real hills/

mountains. Then it should be smooth sailing.

Anyway, back to Paul's visit. The first night was good. We even drank some hot chocolate. We hit the hay around 8 (got in tents around 7 I think). Around 7:30, a few people scouted out our campsite with headlights blaring. It was a little annoying. Luckily, they didn't try to squeeze into our site and they moved a little further north. I'm not sure who it was.

The next morning we started pretty early so we'd have a good amount of time in town/at the hostel in Andover. Terrain wasn't bad and we got picked up at the road around 3pm. Bear from the Cabin picked us up. I think the guy is a dummy. Instead of driving us directly to Grafton Notch to get Paul's car as planned, he insisted on taking us back to the Cabin. So whatever, we went back. Almost immediately after getting there, Don, the guy I originally talked to on the phone, pops out and asks Bear why he didn't take us right to Grafton. So Bear was just clueless. He went inside + Don drove us to Paul's car.

Don is the owner (Honey's) son and Bear is Honey's husband. So I think Bear + Don have a weird relationship.

I need to continue tomorrow—too tired.

October 1 Notes: I failed to understand a lot about the Cabin— too much to even say. Honey and Bear, who are elderly, take complete strangers into their home: they shuttle them all over Maine, they feed them, they listen to them, and they care for them. I was callous in my assessment of the hostel and its caretakers. But more importantly, I was callous in my assessment of these people as individuals. All three—Honey, Bear, and Don—are Trail Angels, and they deserve to be treated as such. I hope if I ever make it back to Andover, the Cabin takes me in a second time as kindly as it took me in the first. Like I said, I am not proud of every entry in this journal.

10-2

Cooper Brook Falls Lean-to: 2126.2

Finally have some time to write. Just got to the shelter and took a quick dip in the swimming hole. It was cold but nice. And I actually feel a little bit clean.

Anyway, back to the Cabin. Me and Paul got there, then got driven to the car, about 30 minutes away. Don told us about a cool microbrewery near where he dropped us off. I think it was called Summer Spring Brewery. Or something Spring Brewery. We went there for a late lunch/early dinner. Had a few beers and some awesome nachos. It was a cool place—good food too. Then we headed back to the Cabin. There were no bunks left (they only have like 6 I think), so me and Paul got a hilarious old, moldy camper to sleep in. It was pretty nasty, but it was a place to sleep. Scratch was there—he was posted up in another old dirty camper.

One thing I forgot about Scratch. I was planning on going into Lincoln with him, but when the hitch wasn't looking good I pulled a mini resupply at some visitor center. But I was still lacking bread and peanut butter—killer. But he was nice enough to give me like 6 pitas and the rest of his peanut butter to get me to Gorham. It was a small thing—but it was nice. He's a good guy. Then I hit the trail and he hitched into Lincoln. He used to go there as a kid to his aunt's place, so he wanted to definitely revisit it.

Back to Paul though. After we settled into our camper we drove to town to see what was there—nothing. There are two general stores and a small diner/restaurant. It's hilarious. We got some snacks + beers at the store then went to the restaurant for all you can eat pizza + salad. It was actually really good. And you got a cookie too.

Then we headed back, watched a couple movies with other hikers + drank some beers. Paul got to meet Trucker, Scratch, Grits, + Sweets which was good. Then there were a bunch of hikers I don't care much for. It was a fun night though—glad Paul got to meet some people.

The next day, Paul hiked a few more miles before heading back to his car. We almost didn't hike at all that day. It was pouring in the morning. So we had an awesome breakfast —eggs, pancakes, sausage, coffee, OJ—then hung around for a bit for the rain to pass. We got out around 1pm to the trail. We got lost trying to find the trailhead for a while! It all worked out though.

Paul did an awesome job hiking. Probably could have done more miles, but I played it a little safe. Fun weekend though and I think Paul had fun.

After Paul left the weather turned pretty bad for a few days. Rainy + cold—not fun. I'm glad it was nice while he was there. The next few days were pretty miserable, I just kept trudging through. I made it to Stratton a few days later—cool town. I wanted to get my own room, but they were booked up, so settled for the hostel at the motel which wasn't bad at all. My original plan was to zero there, but Indy, Patches, + Hotshot texted me saying they were only a couple days ahead, so I pushed on. I won't catch them for the summit, but will see them in Millinocket after. Stratton was cool though. I hung out with Munchies, we had some beers + pizza. I ate some good food at the White Wolf. The next day I wanted to update my blog one last time before summiting, but I couldn't upload pictures. So I wound up burning a morning (library opened at 1pm), and not getting a big post up. I just kind of put up a little one. But that's ok, I'll update soon. I still got in 10 miles that day, but had to hike 'til about 8:30pm—I hate night hiking. It was worth it though. I'm still on track to meet Mom + Dad on Saturday, then summit on Sunday. Just need to hope for good weather.

But my scariest wildlife experience happened just before Stratton. I'll retell here, but see diagram. First let me cook before it gets dark, then I'll write.

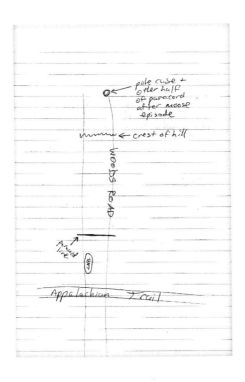

Ok. So the night or two before I got into Stratton I camped on what the guide refers to as a woods road. They're always different—some are used automobile paths, some are just old paths, etc. So I camped there as it was getting dark—there were no other good spots around. But I was afraid of getting run over in the middle of the night by some drunk Mainiac riding a truck or a quad or something down the road. So after some thought, I decided to string my paracord across the road, a bit before my tent, and then hang some stuff on it so you could see I was there. Also, see diagram, I was just below the crest of a hill. So if someone was flying over the hill, they wouldn't see me in time if it was just my tent—hence the paracord maneuver. I hung a few things on it—my white bandana, my socks, my tent case, and my pole case. It turned out pretty well—I think you'd be able to see it decently in headlights.

So I went to bed happy with my creativity. But just as I was curling up, I thought about the woods road again, and how it looked a bit like a game trail. Me + Paul had seen two moose (male + female) a couple days before, and they're scary big. But I shrugged the thought off + went to bed.

Well right around midnight I hear what sounds like a gorilla coming up the road toward me in the direction of the top of the hill. It's kind of this throaty, guttural "uh" every few seconds. Damn it—it's a moose, and it sounds big. In my sleepy haze, everything else happened quickly. I heard the moose, then I didn't, then I heard a tree break, then nothing. I'm obviously terrified at this point. I know the thing was, and maybe still is, very close. I thought I heard the tree snap back across the other side of the trail, but I was wrong.

So all that happens, then nothing. I thought maybe I spooked the moose and he ran into the woods, breaking a tree in the process. But I was terribly wrong.

After hearing the moose once more in the night, I woke up alive + in one piece.

My senses in the night had been wrong, I quickly realized. Getting out of my tent, I noticed my paracord warning mechanism was gone. I found two socks + the tent case on the ground, but no paracord + no pole case. That's when I realized what happened. Going over to the tree I tied the cord to, I saw it crinkled up, partially wrapped around the tree, as if someone pulled it real tight, then let it go. Then I noticed the frayed end. The damn moose snapped the paracord. This stuff is like 500 or 600 pound test—snapped in half. I went to the other tree that I tied off to… and it was gone. The tree was gone. Now it wasn't a big tree. Maybe 2 or 3 inch diameter, but it was still a tree. So I was baffled, and I needed my pole case! So after packing everything up, I searched for a few minutes and found the case about 80 yards up the hill. And next to it I found the half of the paracord still tied to the tree! Holy guacamole.

So here's what I think happened. Moose is just walking down his path, runs into my paracord, snaps the cord in twain, part gets stuck in his rack, he continues on, breaks tree off, drags tree by paracord up the hill 80 yards where it somehow comes off. And this all happened about 10 feet from me. Terrifying.

The next morning, about a mile into the day, I spotted and got an amazing picture of a huge bull moose. Maybe, just maybe, it was the one I almost captured the night before. I'm just glad he wasn't smart enough to know I was in the tent right next to him. I think he would have trampled me to death. In any case, I survived. But that was terrifying! I'll be ok if I don't see any more moose this trip.

Now, on to the next topic. The hike from Stratton to Monson was fairly uneventful. I hiked most of it with Munchies which was cool. I ate a lot of pop tarts. And probably the coolest part was going over the Kennebec River.

The official route of the AT is over the Kennebec via a "ferry." The ferry is really just a canoe that shuttles hikers across from like 9-11am and 2-3pm every day. Or something like that. I got to the river at 9 and was on the first boat. This crazy guy named Hillbilly Dave is the ferryman. Super cool guy. He said he's been the ferryman for about 7 years or so. Me and some yellow blazer (Whiz I think) were on the first boat. Dave was in back, Whiz middle, and I was in front helping Dave row + steer. It was fun. Got to row a bit, then beach the boat into the other side. It was only about a 3 minute ride, but it was awesome.

I'm getting sleepy. I covered a lot today though. I still need to write about: Monson, Tangy, Rebekah + the Lakeshore House, John.

But I must write later. Night.

October 2 Notes: With this entry, I was nearly caught up in my journal. I was only a few days from summiting Katahdin, and I had only the last trail town, Monson, to recount.

Starting just a bit before Stratton, I started to hit another bubble of hikers, primarily made up of yellow blazers who were surging toward the summit of Katahdin before October fifteenth. This second bubble was different from the one that I hit around New York (the one including Mailman, Uke, Lost and Found, Smiley, Dr. Suess, MacGyver, etc.). Along with people like me, Indy, Hotshot, Patches, and Munchies, the hikers in the New York bubble followed the white blazes of the Appalachian Trail. We did not skip parts of the trail. We moved on foot to where we had to get to. We did not jump around, shuttling from trail town to trail town, skipping monstrous chunks of the trail in search of booze or drugs. We were hikers, so we hiked.

Unfortunately, the same can't be said of the bubble of yellow blazers I ran into. They were out there more for the parties than for the trail. As their name implies, these hikers don't follow the white blazes that mark the trail. They follow the yellow streaks of paint that run down the middle of highways—they shuttle a lot and hike a little. And they are good at giving other hikers a bad name. They never bothered me, so I didn't bother them. But being around them wasn't where I wanted to be. I avoided them whenever possible. Theirs wasn't the culture that I came to know and expect from the AT community. It wasn't how I liked to hike and it wasn't the way I wanted to carry myself. So like I said, they can do things their own way—it just wasn't my way.

10-3
Wadleigh Stream Lean-to: 2147.7

Crazy. I am on my last page of the guidebook. I've looked at that page so many times, and now I'm on it. Weird to be this close. My body is ready to be done though. My feet + knees have started to ache a little since the Whites.

Today was decent. My toes were hurting though. I think because my shoes are so worn, my toes are splaying even more than normal, so the flesh between the tip of my toe pad and the pad of my foot is contacting ground a lot. So I have a little soreness there which is weird. But splaying toes are good—so that's ok.

I met Tails + No Name today. Tails is the moron 30 yr old woman who laughs like the Nanny. Rebekah from Lakeshore House hates her. Rebekah caught her smoking in the attic room of the hostel when she wasn't even staying there. Anyway, she's pretty annoying.

But about Monson. That was a cool little town. I pretty much hung at Lakeshore House all day (got in at like noon— started hiking at 4am). And who's the first person I see when I arrive? None other than Tangy! Yes, hilarious. I finally caught the son of a gun. It was great to see him and hang the day. Munchies was there too—so we had the old crew back together. Tangy zeroed there the next day though, so I'm ahead of him. Hope to see him in Millinocket.

But the Lakeshore House was great. Good little bar, good food. And it's right on the lake, so it has an awesome backyard zone. They also have some kayaks you can just take out whenever and zoom around.

The owner Rebekah was awesome too. She did everything at that place (except cook I guess). She was the hostel keeper + the bartender. The few days prior to my arrival, a bunch of hikers raged for Uncle Buck's birthday or something like that. Most were just yellow blazing morons, so Rebekah had her hands full. When I arrived she was pretty pissed. Apparently the hikers were all just being terrible—bad tips, inconsiderate, smoking everywhere, puking in the bathroom, etc. So Rebekah obviously wasn't happy.

But by the end of the night she was. She told us all that we brought her back hope that hikers are good. We pretty much just hung at the bar + partied with her. Tangy had a lot to do with her turnaround—she loved him. Who else was there? Me, Tangy, Munchies, Guru, Acorn, Caveman, and some others including this guy John who I later hiked a bit with.

Overall, it was an awesome town and a cool place. I wish Paul + Matt had got towns like that. But oh well.

So the next morning I lollygagged around with Munchies and Tangy before leaving them. I hope to see them both at the end. I hiked about 15 that day, and so began the 100 Mile Wilderness.

That night I met John. He's just some middle aged dude, fun guy to hike with. He started at the end of February! But he said his time on trail hasn't been that long—he just had to keep going home for stuff. I left him 2 nights ago and have been on target to meet Mom + Dad in 2 days. Crazy.

The Wilderness has been kind of cool. Saw Katahdin from a distance today for the first time—it's pretty enormous. So all I have left is about a 20 tomorrow, then a 13 to meet Mom + Dad, then 5 to the summit. So only about 40 or so more. Weird.

I guess that's all I have to write about now. Probably going to turn in soon + get a good sleep before my last biggish day. Farewell.

October 3 Notes: I'm glad I wasn't in Monson for Uncle Buck's birthday party. Uncle Buck is a guy who began thru-hiking earlier that season (a bit before I started my thru-hike), but got injured somewhere down South. Instead of just leaving the trail, he became a Trail Angel, shuttling hikers around as he followed us northward. I met him a few times here and there, but never got to know him well. He became a bit of a cult figure along the trail: a cheerleader and a mascot. Many hikers used him for his shuttling service. He was a big help to a lot of people when they wanted to get somewhere. He was a pretty neat guy—rotund and always wearing brightly colored shirts. He sported a pink mohawk most of the way. It wasn't that I didn't want to celebrate his birthday, it was that I didn't want to celebrate it with the crowd that was there.

Monson was the beginning of the end. The bite of Autumn let us all know it. The pond was like glass. I understood that this was my last town, my last break from the trail, the last place to see buddies and hang before it was all over. To have a few beers and a few laughs with Munchies and Tangy, who returned to the trail early August in Dalton, was special. I recounted everything in the entry, so no use saying it all again. I left Monson with a heavy heart while they stayed behind. I would summit without them, but I promised myself that Monson would not be the last time I saw them.

I entered the expanse of land called the 100 Mile Wilderness. It was a time to reflect on the entire trail experience: to think, to remember, and to wonder. I spent a lot of time alone during the Wilderness, but I'm glad John was around me too. John was a slightly older man, but he moved like a high schooler. He was lengthy, sinewy, and strong. He rolled his own cigarettes and drank beers whenever he had the chance. He felt like an old friend, grown up and trapped in an old man's body. His presence kept me grounded during what was a silently emotional last leg of the trail. He became someone to count on in spirit when words didn't count for much. We never really talked too much about the end of the trail, or anything substantial for that matter. But I think we could both feel it—our spirits rested upon and bolstered each other. Like Indy, John reflected back to me my own feelings, and he let me look upon the entire journey from a higher point of view.

10-4

Hurd Brook Lean-to: 2167.3

Well I guess this is the last real night in the woods. Tomorrow night will be at the Birches, kind of the Katahdin staging area. I think it's finally sinking in that I'm at the end—only about 18 miles.

I just met a guy who's just out for a few days—Glen Gordon. He's planning on thru hiking next year. It's weird that I'm now the one people thinking about thru hiking look to for advice/questions/etc.

It has been an awesome journey. It kind of feels like just yesterday that I was in my room prepping all of my stuff. And now I'm almost done already.

I'm not really sure how to feel right now. I'm ready to be done but I'm not. It will be so bittersweet to climb Katahdin.

I'm not sure what the future holds after this trip. I'm both excited + scared for it. This trip has been such a departure from "normal" life. No one to answer to but myself. No schedule but my own. No plans but the ones I set. It's such a liberating experience to have that. And under my own plans

+ power, I've made it here. I'm just afraid back in "real" life that I'll have more to answer to than myself—and that's normally when I fail or struggle or become unhappy. There is so much pressure from everyone but myself to "succeed" in life. It all seems so backwards. When I have no one but myself to set my goals, I always exceed them. For some reason, I can't live up to the success standards of the modern world. And I'm afraid when I return, I'll once again be floundering to find my place in life and find "success."

So I don't know what to do. I don't know what to be or how to be it.

I've answered a good amount of my questions out here —or at least got a good start on them. But so many more questions arise when you answer one. I think we'll just never be able to figure it all out. We don't have the insight or the brain power to see it all. And I'm ok with that. I just feel like the world demands answers. But I can't give an answer—we don't know. Everyone thinks they know—but they don't know anything. We're not physiologically capable of answering the big questions. So we get caught up in the little questions. We make all our lives about the little things. And I'm tired of that. I want to struggle with the big questions and fail. I don't want to think I know about the little things even when I don't.

I'm just rambling now. But honestly, I'm scared for the future. I don't want to forget the things I've thought out here, and I don't want to return to the world of little things. I'm tired of acting professionally, moving objects, and calling it work. That is work of a lesser calling.

I just hope this experience reverberates. I hope it was as good for everyone, and for the world, as it was for me.

Who knows what the future holds. I have felt the cessation of time and the passage of time in one. I need to keep looking for that. I can't get caught up in time forever. I need to remember the cessation of time as well. I need to remember the freedom. I need to make all of this count.

Well tomorrow I have an early hike to meet Mom + Dad. It will be weird. I'm looking forward to it. I need to sleep now.

Talk to you soon weirdos.

October 4 Notes: This is my last journal entry for quite a long time. My delay in writing is not due to fatigue, as was often the case. I summited, as planned, the morning of October 7. But the fact that I had finished my adventure took some time to sink in.

The time I had from this entry to my next was a time to allow my emotions to settle. I would leave the way of life I had lived for the past five months and return home to South Jersey. I would leave behind friends I made and places I had come to love. And it would take a while for me to understand: what I had done, who I had met, what I had seen. During this time, I slowly went from feeling that I lived a dream in which I summited Katahdin, to realizing that I was finished—it was all real, and it was all over.

10-22-13

Summit Day Plus Sixteen: New Jersey

So this will be my last journal entry. Before I get into some stuff, let me recollect what happened on Summit Day.

The night before Summit Day was a tough sleep. I was awake a decent amount of the time. It was just a strange feeling to be at the campground, in a lean-to, with families vacationing around me. It was clear that this was the end of the trail. No more open wilderness + woods + lakes. It was just campground + Katahdin. That was all I had left. And in my restless sleep, I knew that.

I woke early, before my alarm sounded. I packed up my gear, got water, + walked to the Ranger station to leave my pack there. I would summit with just my day pack. I would enjoy these last few miles, not struggle through them.

The first mile or two was easy. I passed by Whirled Peas + her fiance. The middle two miles or so were a rapid ascent. It was a fun climb though, especially with a day pack. I saw Uke as well. He was with two friends. I passed them by. After getting above treeline, it was beautiful. You could just turn around at any time and get an amazing view of the land. Several times I just sat + watched—no rush.

One of the funny parts of the ascent was when I passed two day hiking girls, around my age. One had obviously hiked before, and the other had obviously not hiked much at all. The latter was having a breakdown. "What? What do I do? How do people do this?! How do people get down!?"

Granted, it was a tough climb. There were several spots where you had to do some weird moves with the rebar in the rocks. But I had a blast at least! I watched them as I climbed, and they seemed to be doing ok.

After the steep climb, you hit the tabletop—the last mile or so of the AT. When I reached Thoreau Spring, I was slightly disappointed. I saw water flowing over the trail, but couldn't find the spring source. I sat and rested here—my last break before completion. I thought of how many times I had looked at this place in my guide book—Thoreau Spring. I had dreamed of getting to this place, and now I was here. At the sign post, I learned that Thoreau climbed Katahdin. It was pretty inspiring to be in the place where one of my heroes once was. Walden was one of the first books I read about living a non-conformist life. And its lessons + spirit have stuck with me since I read it—junior year at UD. So I relished the chance to stand at Thoreau Spring, one mile from the summit. Three other day hiking dudes were there though. Their pushups + cheesy conversation were a bit of a downer. So with a glance at the marker, I turned toward the peak.

I didn't look up too much during the last mile. Honestly, I didn't want it to end. I didn't even want to see the end. But my body kept going. My mind whirled with memories of the trip. Is it possible that all that happened in five months? How was that five months? Time did not pass normally. In the normal world, time seems to act consistently. But on the trail, time seemed almost like something non-existent. The experience seems to me now like one bulk perspective. Things did not happen chronologically, they simply happened.

About 100 yards from the top I saw John. He was going back down after his summit. My head was whirling, and I'm sure his was too. We talked briefly, congratulated each other, and parted. I forgot to offer him a ride into town, and forgot to offer him some whiskey.

Next thing I knew, I was approaching the summit signboard. I approached slowly, and scoped out the view. I didn't want to go up + touch the board yet. I felt that that would signal the end. And I didn't want it to end. So I talked to some guy about the Yanks, then stood alone. I walked toward the board + reached out + touched it. That was it. I had done it. I walked it all—from Georgia to Maine. I was a thru-hiker, but my journey was now done. That was it. I didn't feel much emotion. I felt dulled. I felt dislocated. Some guy took my picture. I thanked him, then walked off a little bit to get somewhat alone (there were way more people up there than I thought there'd be). I sat down + just thought. Emotion welled up in me after I sent a text to the siblings—"Harry, I've reached the top!"

I sat and cried a bit. Yup, I did. Whirled Peas + her fiance came up behind me then. We shared congrats + disbelief that we were done. We shared a couple swigs of whiskey as well.

Team Hustle + Flow made it up then too. As I was taking their summit photos, Mom + Dad made it up the Saddle! It was great to see them. Oh yea, I opened up my gifts before they got up there. Cards + a shirt from the siblings. It was nice.

I took my pictures, drank some whiskey, and shared the moment with Ma + Pa. We hung at the peak for maybe 45 minutes. Then it was time to leave + to be done.

Ma + Dad had an adventure getting to the peak. Instead of the 3 miles up (like we thought) it was actually 6 to the top. But they gutted it out, especially over the steep 1 mile stretch. They did well—they gutted it big time.

It took a while to get back down to the car. We finished at maybe 4 or so. With the hiking done, it was time to hit the town!

I'll write about town later tonight. Ma + Gram just got back from the store.

October 22 Notes: The summiting of Katahdin felt overwhelmingly final, yet not fully real. Tears started forming in my eyes during the walk from Thoreau Spring to the top. I wanted to be back in Georgia with Tangy and Munchies. I wanted to be in Pennsylvania with Indy, Hotshot, and Patches. I wanted to be in Vermont with Scratch and Trucker. I didn't want to be done. I wish I had asked John to come back up with me, to talk about what just happened, and what we would do next. But I couldn't think. I wasn't sure what to do. I conversed blankly with the man about the Yankees. I looked out: the sky was blue, the earth brown and green. I looked at all of the tourists and day hikers who shared the end with me. They didn't understand what was happening to me: I was atop a mountain I had wanted to conquer for five months, but I felt as though I were the one being destroyed. I wanted the mountain to support me, but it fell away on all sides. I stared at the weathered, battered signboard without seeing the white words. I touched it. I wished no one was there so I could cry out loud.

My goal for the last five months, the only thing I was driving toward, was now done—and I missed it as though a loving memory of the distant past had slipped away forever. And I still miss it now. I can still picture parts of the trail so vividly. I can picture specific rocks, logs, campsites, certain smudges of dirt, certain bars and seats and beds in hostels, certain cuts and blisters and blood, specific smiles and faces and beards and eyes, certain signposts and arrows and markings, and certain views atop mountains and of streams with no names—Katahdin is but one of those things I remember. It will forever be lodged in my mind as the end of a journey that allowed me to annihilate the path I thought I had to take. I am free. My life is changed forever.

Coming down off of Katahdin was like being cast out of Heaven. I knew I could never attain that experience again—those people, those places, and those experiences are forever locked away and sanctified. They are relics for me now—to be revered, remembered, and smiled upon when I pull them from the cabinets of my mind.

Epilogue: 11-1-13

"Driven by the forces of love, the fragments of the world seek each other so that the world may come into being."

—Pierre Teilhard de Chardin

So let me recap my time in Millinocket after Summit Day. First off, Millinocket is a hilarious town—there really isn't much to do there.

The first night, we crashed pretty early after eating dinner. Mom + Dad were spent. And Dad banged his toe pretty bad on the hike. So as usual, he handled bodily injury horribly. He thought he'd need an amputation. He was a mental mess.

So that night was just a few beers + sleep.

Over the next couple days, we did a lot of eating + drinking. Like I said, not much to do in Millinocket. We asked our B+B guy what we can do. He said 1) mini golf place that is literally never open 2) drive an hour to an antique tool museum 3) drive multiple hours to try to find a moose. We did none of those things.

We did visit some shops in town which was fun. Mom got a couple funny signs about wine. One was "This may be the wine talking, but I love wine." I thought that one was funny. The second night, we hung at the Blue Ox with Indy, Haley, + The Voice. It was the first time I met the Voice, so it was cool. It was awesome to see Indy again before it was all over. We had a fun, raucous night. The next day, they would head out. And that's the last I've seen of Indy.

The next night (Mom + Dad's last), we hung with Tangy, Munchies + some random dude named Scarecrow. It was a blast seeing Tangy + Munchies again. Mom + Dad loved them. We got some good pictures + had a good time.

They all had not summited yet though. The next day they set out on the trail to summit on Wednesday.

And just like that, my friends were gone. I had one more day + night in town before the end.

Most of the day I blogged. As I was walking to dinner, from out of the cafe I heard someone call my name—Trucker! He had just summited along with Lady Mac + Snacks. I was glad to run into them. I had dinner with them + Lady Mac's + Snack's families. Snack's dad bought for me which was really nice. We had a few beers, then Snacks + Lady Mac had to hit the road.

I met up a little later with Trucker at the Blue Ox where we had a hilarious night with some crazy drunk locals. It was fun hanging with Trucker. Before I knew it, the night was done. I walked to the B+B down the middle of the road—there wasn't a soul around.

Luckily, I saw one more guy I wanted to see—John. My last morning, I ran into him + his wife at the cafe. We only spoke briefly, but I'm glad I ran into him.

A few hours later, my B+B guy was driving me to the airport. So that was it. My post-summit celebration was done. I can't explain how glad I am that I was able to see my buddies (especially Tangy, Munchies, + Indy) before we went our separate ways. If I hadn't it would have felt like the loop was still open. In a way, I hope it still is—maybe I'll hang with those guys sometime down the line.

The people really do make the trail. It would be a totally different place without the people. As I'm back in normal life, I keep thinking of the trail + all the great people on it. It's a great place, but the individuals are what amplify the physical beauty of the trail. The matter + spirit amplify each other beautifully on the trail and I'm glad my mind was there to perceive it all.

It's difficult to sum up the trail. It is a temporal experience, but it's also more than that. My mind and perspective have been altered, hopefully permanently and for the better. A more simplified life is a more beautiful life. A physical struggle fills a space in the mind. And new friends are always welcome.

I don't know where I'll wind up in a month or two, or even in five or ten years. But I do know I want to be happy. I don't think I'll ever be a rich man, because I don't need it. There is a lot more to the world than the successful acquisition of wealth. I'd prefer to spend my days in the acquisition of experience, love, + creation. If that means monetary minimalism, I'm ok with that.

For whoever reads this, including myself, one of the biggest things to remember is this: Experiences like this help us to learn. But they will never answer all the questions. Humanity needs to humble itself in the big questions. But we can still feel great things, even if we can't answer them. So strive to learn continually, but know that you may never get the answers—you may only get the love.

Fare thee well my friends.

Appendix

Alone: A Blog Entry

So a lot of people are kind of baffled, or weirded out when I tell them that I hike alone. They ask me how I do that—how I spend all that time by myself, utterly alone. My standard cookie cutter answer (you tend to have a lot of them in your back pocket when you hike the AT—it's not a bad thing, you just get a lot of the same questions) is something like, "Well I'm not alone all the time. There are people that kind of bounce in and out, and you see them here and there. And you hike a little bit with them. But yea, for the most part you are alone."

But the deeper truth is something a bit more difficult to articulate in thirty seconds to the questioner. The deeper truth is much more difficult for me even to understand, even though I know it to be true.

I've struggled over writing this post for some time now. And I didn't want to write it too early, because I wanted to make sure what I was thinking and feeling was not of a whim. So bear with me as I try to write this down. It may not come across as eloquently and clearly as I have thought it through in my head. But hopefully some sense, at least, comes through.

The deeper truth is that I am not alone. Yes, there are times when I do feel isolated. Not physical isolation—that I can deal with. I'm talking about platonic isolation. I feel, in effect, isolated and alone in my core. One of the most memorable times this happened was the day after Solitaire and Scuba Springsteen left. I missed home a bit, and I missed my friends and family, and I was a ways behind my trail friends. It was a rough day. So yes, there are definitely tough times at some points. But more importantly, those times are fleeting, and they are few. They are a rut in the mind to be broken out of. They are something to be thought on, understood, and then overcome.

I know there is a deeper knowledge and a deeper truth that I sometimes understand when I am out there. It is not often, and it is as fleeting as my sad times, but it is more true.

Even in physical loneliness, there is sometimes a frame of mind that I see through that shows me that I am never alone. It is difficult to explain in text, or articulate in words, but it is there. When you have a lot of time to think about the world, and the cosmos, and what every thing, every object, every piece of matter, is in the world, you come to see something deeper than these 'things.' There is something more, something that resembles more of nothingness, that is part of everything and not part of anything. But it is the one thing the whole of our beings, and the whole of the cosmos share in common. It is not love as we know it today, but it is an energy that we all share. An understanding of empathy that we, along with every other piece of creation, are all part of this experience that we understand as the unfolding universe.

So when I first started my journey, I took my Grandfather's Yanks hat with me. It was kind of a memento—something to hold on to on tougher days. And it was a way to keep my Grandfather with me who passed away a couple of years ago. But as I've thought of these things more, and the place of mere matter like a Yankees hat, I've come to understand that I don't need the hat to have my Grandfather.

We always tend to focus on 'some thing' nowadays in order to be happy or find a solution. Initially for me, it was my Grandpa's hat. But what I've found is that things are not the answer. There is this amazing 'no thing' that binds each and every piece of creation in the cosmos. A nothing that was there before the cosmos came into being, and will be there when it is over. And that great Nothingess is what we all share and what we all somehow experience, in one way or another. It's an amazing paradox that doesn't make sense—I know it doesn't make sense. But I love it for what it is. It's a chance to experience what we have in front of us, to cherish every piece of matter, every object we come to know, but to also realize that all these things somehow sprung forth out of a nothingness. It's a great feeling when I am able to wrap my mind around it—this connection that all things have. But like I said, I only see it sometimes, in beautifully fleeting moments.

So why do I hike alone? I don't hike alone—nobody does. Nobody lives alone, nobody dies alone, nobody does anything alone. We're all part of something amazing, the monumental journey of the universe itself. You can not walk alone in such an extraordinary event —it is impossible.

Thanks

A very special thanks goes out to my mother and father, both of whom have supported me through all of my crazy hopes, dreams, and adventures. It is a fact that I would not have had many of the greatest experiences of my life had it not been for your love and support. I can write only so much with words. They will never attain the depth of my gratitude. Thanks to my family and friends back home, in Mount Laurel, Hoboken, and everywhere else. Your interest, support, and love as I hiked the trail were enormous for me. Once I had so many people following my trip, I knew I couldn't stop! You guys kept my spirits high, and let me know that no matter where I go, I always have home. Thanks to my brothers and sister for spending time with me on the trail and being a part of my life. Having you be a part of my experience is special. I'll always remember that. And a huge thanks to Paul for making the cover to my book. Thanks to Leah for all your love and support. You are my best friend love. And thanks to Brandon "Monkey" Imp and Steve "Scuba Springsteen" Olson. I picked your guys' brains for all the information I could get about thru-hiking, and you came through. I appreciate your help and patience.

To my trail friends: many aspects of the trail are difficult to sum up, especially the community and humanity I encountered. Five months is not a very long time, but it is amazing how many rich experiences I had with you all in that time. I can not thank you all enough for making my trip an amazing time in my life. Each of you has become a part of me, and I truly appreciate that.

To anyone who has taken the time to read about my trip. Many thru-hikers chronicle their adventure for others, so it is an honor for me to have you read through my personal journey when there are so many out there. I can't thank you enough.

And lastly, to everyone, everywhere, who is a stooge. Stay weird.

Sincerely—
Chris Quinn
The Esteemed Stooge, Sir Charles Guilons

Thru-Hikers and Section Hikers:

Acorn
AO
Bahalana
Boo Bear
Bud
Cannon
Caveman Chris
Cedric
Chipmunk
Colonel Patches
Conundrum
Data
Dimples
Dream Catcher
Dr. Suess
Eyes
Fiddlehead
Fire Hydrant
Frosty
Scratch
Grits
Guru
Hail Satan (aka Beelzebub)
Hostel Talker
Hotshot
Hummingbird
Inch Worm
Juno
Jupiter
Lady
Lady Mac
Let's Party (aka Party)
Little Bear
Lost and Found
Lotus
MacGyver
Mailman

Munchies
Music Man
Nine Nails
No Name
Patches
The Pilgrim
Pockets
Poncho
Ripsock
River
Rerun
Rojo
Rusty
Scarecrow
Shaman
Smiley
Snacks
Songbird
Stay Puffed
Stealth
Stretch
Strider
Sunshine
Sweets
Tails
Tangy (aka Tangy Booch Magoo)
Team Hustle and Flow: Etcetera, Fat Toodles, and Raven (aka Rylu)
Tennessee
Uke
Uno
Wash
Whirled Peas
Whisper
Whiz
Willow
Wood Elf
Wooden Spoon

Non Thru-Hikers:

Aunt Reen—Aunt from Glen Allen, VA
Bahm—Hometown friend
Brandon Imp (aka Monkey)—High school classmate, former thru-hiker
Celli—Hometown friend, bachelor partier
Cindy—Former co-worker
ClearPoint crew—Former co-workers
Dana—Matt, my brother's wife
Dad
Danielle—My sister
Higgins—Hometown friend, bachelor partier
Elmer—Owner of Elmer's, hiker hostel in Hot Springs, NC
Fagan—Hometown and Hoboken friend, bachelor partier
John—Hoboken friend, owner of Farside
Leah — Hometown friend, rekindled flame, love interest, etc.
Mark—Uncle from Glen Allen, VA
Matt (aka The Googan)—My brother and bachelor partier
Mom
Morgan—Hometown friend
Nan and Pop—My father's parents, from Glen Allen, VA
Paul (aka Solitaire)—My brother and bachelor partier
Rick—Fiance of Cindy
Ron Brown—Trail Angel, drove me from Atlanta to Springer
Steve Olson (aka Scuba Springsteen)—My hometown friend and 2012 thru-hiker
Steve Reynolds—College friend
Taylor (T Man)—Cousin from Glen Allen, VA
Uncle Buck—Trail Angel
Zach—Hometown friend

Section Quotes

Prologue: from The *Divine Milieu* by Pierre Teilhard de Chardin

Part I: from *The Great Work* by Thomas Berry

Part II: from *The Great Work* by Thomas Berry

Epilogue: from *The Phenomenon of Man* by Pierre Teilhard de Chardin

About the Author

Chris Quinn grew up in Mount Laurel, New Jersey. After graduating from the University of Delaware, he lived and worked in Hoboken for a few years before hiking the Appalachian Trail in 2013. He is now a writer and a teacher in South Jersey.

For more of his works and stories, check out www.quinnwriter.com.